PRACTICAL GRACE

Grace for your Whole Life

October 2019

David Orrison

Printed in the United States
First Printing, 2019

Grace for the Heart Publications
PO Box 2882
Loveland, CO 80539
www.gracefortheheart.org

Scripture quotations, unless otherwise noted, are
from the New King James version. (Holy Bible: The
New King James Version. 1982. Nashville: Thomas
Nelson.)

The cover illustration by Harold Copping is in the
public domain. It has been used in many forms and
sold in edited versions. We recognize his contribution to the art of the church by not removing his
name from the painting and using it as it originally
appeared in "Scenes in the Life of our Lord" published
by the Religious Tract Society in 1907.

For my sons

CONTENTS

PREFACE

Over 40 years ago my wife and I were serving in a difficult situation and found ourselves worn out from the struggle. As has been our custom over the years, we wrote a ministry Christmas letter in addition to our usual letter for family and friends. In the ministry letter we asked people to pray and let them know what had been happening in the Lord's work.

That year I wrote that we were tired. It seemed a simple thing to say, something anyone would understand. The ministry had been stressful in many ways. We got back a brief note from Rev. Ralph Chamberlain, who had been the pastor of my home church where I grew up. I don't have the note anymore, but I remember clearly what he said: "You shouldn't be tired if you are doing the Lord's work!"

Well, I confess that I had no idea what he was talking about. It sounded like a spiritual platitude. We didn't find much comfort in his statement and, quite honestly, we continued to be tired in ministry.

But I remembered what Rev. Chamberlain had said! It haunted me; I suppose. Was there truth in those words? Was it possible that I had missed something important in understanding ministry? Of course, some of my tiredness came from physical exhaustion and stress, but there was also something more in it. I was tired spiritually. And... why was I exhausted and stressed?

The crisis passed, and we entered a new ministry, but the seed was planted. Our hearts began to look more to Jesus for strength and fulfillment. We were learning to expect His activity in and through our lives.

After a couple years, the Lord led me to a personal study of what the Scriptures taught about a real relationship with Jesus and the meaning of God's grace. I thought I had heard all these things before, but over time the truths became more real, more substantial. I began to see the same theme throughout Scripture: that Jesus Christ has done and will do His work.

The Lord led me to a good friend and mentor. Bob Bingham is a pastor and counselor, but mostly he leads people to Jesus. No, not as an evangelist, but as a disciple-maker with the right understanding of discipleship. Bob's ministry has been to show believers how to take their eyes off themselves and the attacks of the enemy to focus on the amazing Person of Jesus Christ. Over his long ministry, Bob has been used by the Lord to open the hearts of thousands of believers to a functional relationship with Jesus. As I write this, Bob and Dottie Bingham continue to teach people the true meaning of grace in every part of life through the ministry of CupBearers/Gracestoration in Englewood, Colorado.

Through talking with Bob and through studying the Word of God, I have grown in my understanding of grace in daily living. I continue to be a student, however. Many authors and speakers contributed in various ways to what I have learned. I speak with deep appreciation of Major Ian Thomas and A. W. Tozer. These men brought a special gift to us out of their own relationships with Jesus.

God's grace in Jesus is the key to Christian living and is, perhaps, the deepest of all theological mysteries. Forever, I will marvel at the fact that the Lord of the universe has chosen to reach down to my need with His abundance in the living Person of Jesus Christ! It is my prayer that you will grow through this study into a deeper relationship with Him.

David Orrison, September 2019

WHY THIS BOOK?

I have been a pastor for over 40 years. Over that time, I have worked with people in a wide variety of places on the Christian journey. Almost all of them have struggled with the idea of grace. For most people, grace is nice... just nice. They don't really know what it means or how it affects their lives. The word means little to them.

The real problem with which they struggle is not the word *grace* but the whole idea of God's activity in their lives. They wonder just what part is theirs and what part is God's. They extend their learned ideas of responsibility and duty into the Christian message and produce a broken Christian walk, one that is filled with regrets and guilt and fear.

Perhaps fear is the most common. They wonder whether they have done enough, whether they have lived "good enough." To salve their fear, they add to themselves an ever-increasing regimen of restrictions and works. They identify their sin and resolve to stop it, only to find that it continues, or a new sin begins. They try to add new activities and new habits to combat the sin, but there is little blessing for them in these things. More Bible memory, more kind words, more acts of service; fewer hours with the television, less football or time on the phone... but nothing really helps.

Of course, there are also those who already know, either from hard experience or from some inner sense of personal defeat, that trying harder won't work, so they don't try at all. They simply resign themselves to the idea that life will be full of misery and unfulfilled desires, that they will never really be free of harmful habits, and that God probably just doesn't care. They are Christians, for the most part, but they have little hope or expectation of joy in this life.

Jesus told the parable of the sower and the four different journeys of the seed. We usually say that the seed is the message of the gospel, the way of salvation in Christ. Of course, that is true, but the message of God's grace is the message of the gospel. The parable has a strong application after salvation just as it has prior to salvation.

> *"Listen! Behold, a sower went out to sow. And it happened, as he sowed, that some seed fell by the wayside; and the birds of the air came and devoured it. Some fell on stony ground, where it did not have much earth; and immediately it sprang up because it had no depth of earth. But when the sun was up it was scorched, and because it had no root it withered away. And some seed fell among thorns; and the thorns grew up and choked it, and it yielded no crop. But other seed fell on good ground and yielded a crop that sprang up, increased and produced: some thirtyfold, some sixty, and some a*

hundred." And He said to them, "He who has ears to hear, let him hear!" Mark 4:3-9

The message of God's grace is greater than simply the salvation message. There is something that should happen in the life of the believer. The word is planted in the lives of the hearers, but it often does not grow. Jesus explained the parable when his disciples asked about it.

"The sower sows the word. And these are the ones by the wayside where the word is sown. When they hear, Satan comes immediately and takes away the word that was sown in their hearts. These likewise are the ones sown on stony ground who, when they hear the word, immediately receive it with gladness; and they have no root in themselves, and so endure only for a time. Afterward, when tribulation or persecution arises for the word's sake, immediately they stumble. Now these are the ones sown among thorns; they are the ones who hear the word, and the cares of this world, the deceitfulness of riches, and the desires for other things entering in choke the word, and it becomes unfruitful. But these are the ones sown on good ground, those who hear the word, accept it, and bear fruit: some thirtyfold, some sixty, and some a hundred." Mark 4:14-20

Apparently, fruit is the evidence of success! Those that remain unfruitful have not truly received the word. Too many Christians have received the word of salvation but have no idea what is supposed to happen in their lives afterward. They might get a new list of rules to live by or a pat on the head from those who should lead them to an understanding of grace, but they get little else. Perhaps the saddest truth is that those who have led them to salvation often don't know that there is anything more.

What is the word that is spread? Is it just the way of salvation? No! It is the way of life! It is not enough to say that Jesus died to give us salvation. Jesus died to give us life, and that's what grace is all about. That's the word that is sown.

Some believers hear the word of God's grace, and it is almost immediately stifled by the teaching of those they have chosen to follow. There are teachers today who are binding believers in ways the Pharisees never even considered. I have heard evangelical teachers express the need for Christians to "stop talking about grace and start talking about the law." Some teach that grace is earned by good works, that a believer does not receive grace freely from the Lord. These teachers snatch the hope and promise of God's grace from the hearts of their followers.

Some hear the word of God's grace and receive it with joy, but they have no support and no context in which the idea can grow. They never hear the truth about grace from the pulpit or from their Bible studies, and they have no one to lead them and show them the way. So, their excitement drains away, and they lose the little they had.

Some hear the word of God's grace and receive it with joy but find themselves unable to apply it to their daily lives. The struggles of life overwhelm them, and they set grace aside to tackle their problems on their own. It just doesn't seem right to them to rest in the strength of the Lord when the work pushes itself into their faces.

But there are some—and the number is growing—who are learning that it is God Who does His work, in and through and with them, and it is God Who will carry them through their lives. They are learning to trust Jesus and, in the process, growing deeper in love with Him every day.

It is my prayer that this book will help to lead you to the truth about God's grace in Jesus and that you will find yourself bearing much fruit as you yield your whole life to Him.

GRACE DEFINED

What word is more foundational to the Christian faith than "grace"? It is a word of simple and joyful songs and of the deepest mysteries of theology. On the concept of grace, the Church has discussed and fought and meditated for all her history. Yet, in our day, we seem to have lost the vitality of grace for the Christian life. The word is left to the mystics or the theologians or simply allowed to stay in the atmospheric culture of Christianity with little or no meaning. It is time to reclaim this amazing concept!

When most Christians think of grace, they find themselves entering the dark room of thought and idea. Grace is rarely allowed out of that room to make a difference in the person's life. Yet, grace is a wonderful and life-changing concept when properly understood. In fact, we could say that grace is the most active concept in the true Christian life!

A radical change of thinking must take place in an individual's life before he or she can begin to enjoy the life of grace God has for His people. It is a significant achievement simply to begin to make the distinction between self and Lord, between our own ideas and goals and His ideas and goals. Just to think in those terms is a challenge for most of us. But our plan for this book is to do just that, to change the way we think about grace, to understand its value and activity in our lives.

We are trained to do things for ourselves from the earliest age. Our accomplishments are heralded as something good, and we are honored for them. From that training, we assume that our efforts are to be the focus of our lives. We praise good behavior and punish bad behavior and train ourselves to worship our behavior. We offer our works as the blessing we give to one another, and we even offer our works to our Lord as some special blessing from us to Him.

Although we, as evangelicals, have known that not one of us was saved because of our efforts—our good works—there has been among almost all believers the idea that our good works will keep us in good standing with our Lord. That's part of the thinking that ought to change as we learn more about grace. We must begin to understand that it was completely His work that saved us and that it is completely His effort that keeps us right before our Lord. In other words, nothing of my "self" is worthy of salvation before or after the fact. I have no good works to bring to the Lord or to hold up before any person. The only good works others might see in my life are those things which Jesus does in and through me.

That is fact. It is what the Scriptures teach. He is to be the active force in my life; He must be my life, if I am truly to please the Lord. This change of thinking and the corresponding change of activity will be our goal as we proceed into understanding the role of God's grace in every part of our lives.

There is a remaining question. How can we make this real in our daily lives? Our lives are filled with such practical and daily needs. Relationships, jobs, health, and money: these are the things that dictate so much of our thinking and our activity. Is grace something for those areas of our lives? If it is not, it will remain in the "ivory towers" of theology and not be truly important to us. In other words, does grace make a difference in my marriage or in my relationship with my children? Is grace a consideration when I know that I have done something wrong, whether it was by choice or by accident? Does grace make a difference in those areas of my life to which I have to give most of my concern? If not, then grace has little to offer as a concept for most Christians.

Like Adam, we all lie lifeless on the ground with nothing to offer until God breathes His "functional" life into us. We became alive, not just for salvation but, for daily activity. Did that happen in your life when you became a Christian? If it did, whatever happened to that life? If it didn't, it can!

Over the course of this book I hope to show how any Christian can walk moment by moment by this grace. What you will learn about grace may change your life. After all, the Christian faith is not just a process of endurance until the "good day" comes. There is a life to be lived here and now... and God's grace in Jesus is the substance of that life.

I confess to you that this message comes out of a genuine searching for the answer for my own life. I want the life of Jesus to be real and active in me. I want to get out of His way so that He can do whatever it is He wants to do in me. I want to be so attentive to Him and so available to Him that my simplest actions are led by Him and please Him.

With these things in mind I want to avoid the usual questions from deep theology and get right to the heart of the matter. There are other books about the relationship between grace and law and the historical and theological discussion concerning grace. What I want to do is give us a working and living definition of grace.

I will begin by stating that grace is simply <u>what God does</u>. We could take it another step and say that grace is what God does <u>for us</u>. I believe that this is the proper Scriptural definition of grace. It is obviously simple and is meant to embrace a broad application in our lives, because Christ is active in every part of our lives.

In Harold Copping's illustration of the *Healing of the Leper* (seen on the cover of this book), Jesus bends down to meet the need of the leper. The primary Hebrew word for grace seems to encapsulate this concept. The word is *chane*, which means "to bend down toward another in kindness." There is another word which, I believe, corresponds to this. It is the word, *Canaan*, which means to be humbled. We will come back to that.

I have seen dozens of famous paintings and illustrations of the healing of the leper. Few, if any, capture the brokenness of the leper of biblical times. Covered with oozing sores, hiding behind rags, abhorrent to any who saw him, this man bowed before Jesus in his great need. He had nothing to offer, no beauty or privilege or wealth. Rejected by all the people, the leper represents the most pitiable.

The concept of grace taught by the Bible is that the Lord, in His power and majesty, in His wisdom and love, bends down to us in our brokenness and humility to provide all our needs. That's grace.

And the Scripture says,

> *But Noah found grace in the eyes of the LORD.*
> *Gen 6:8*

In a broken and depraved world, Noah opened his heart to the Lord and found grace. He found the love of God for His people. He found the way of salvation.

Again, years later, the children of Israel escaped Egypt by the grace of God only to disobey Him and spend the next forty years wandering. At the end of their wandering, as they are about to enter the land of promise, Moses tells them the reason for their suffering.

> *And you shall remember that the LORD your God led you all the way these forty years in the wilderness, to humble you and test you, to know what was in your heart, whether you would keep His commandments or not. So He humbled you, allowed you to hunger, and fed you with manna which you did not know nor did your fathers*

> *know, that He might make you know that man*
> *shall not live by bread alone; but man lives by every*
> *word that proceeds from the mouth of the LORD.*
> *Deuteronomy 8:2-3*

Remember the word mentioned earlier that meant being broken or humbled? *Canaan*, the name of the Promised Land. There is an important lesson just in the name of the land. The people of God were delivered from their slavery and humiliation in Egypt so they could live a humble and broken life before the Lord. If they did this, if they remembered that it was His power, His wisdom, His love, which had delivered them and would always sustain them, if they remembered to be humble before Him, He would make something great of them. He would use them to tell the world of His love. He would protect them and provide for them, and they would have more joy than they could imagine—if they were humble before Him.

It is important to understand that God is under obligation to no one. He is God, and there is no other. No one deserves His grace. No one is entitled to His grace. His grace is always a gift of love, of compassion. Never forget that. There is no ritual, no work, nothing anyone can do to force Him to give His grace. It is His decision alone.

> *Then He said, "I will make all My goodness pass be-*
> *fore you, and I will proclaim the name of the LORD*
> *before you. I will be gracious to whom I will be gra-*
> *cious, and I will have compassion on whom I will*
> *have compassion."*

Exodus 33:19

And the message is that grace comes to the humble, to the broken. Grace is the powerful and loving Lord reaching down to His hurting people to provide all their needs. Listen to the Scriptures:

> *But He gives more grace. Therefore He says: "God resists the proud, but gives grace to the humble." James 4:6*

Only the humble can receive grace.

> *Thus says the LORD: "Heaven is My throne, And earth is My footstool. Where is the house that you will build Me? And where is the place of My rest? For all those things My hand has made, and all those things exist," says the LORD. "But on this one will I look: On him who is poor and of a contrite spirit, and who trembles at My word." Isaiah 66:1-2*

There are many verses that support this. God blesses those who come to Him in repentance and brokenness. That brings up two very important questions. First, just what does repentance and brokenness mean? If this is so important, we need to understand it.

The broken and contrite heart belongs to a person who has examined his or her life and has understood his or her need. When we look at ourselves and see how far short of God's plan we fall, we are humbled.

David certainly exhibits this brokenness in the 51st Psalm. Confronted with his sin, he knows what to do. He turns his heart in humility to the Lord. You can almost picture David on his knees as he prays this prayer of repentance. He cannot ignore the truth of his sin. He cannot bargain with God or redefine terms or blame someone else. He doesn't even try these things. Instead, he humbles himself. He agrees with God on his unworthiness and he looks to God for mercy and strength.

To be humble and broken before the Lord is to throw yourself on His mercy, to depend on Him for everything. It is to be the man in Copping's illustration, bowing continually before the only One who has what you need.

The second question is "How?" How can we do this? For most of us there are rare times when we are bowed down before the Lord, but this is not the normal or natural thing in our lives. In fact, it is easiest for us to fall back on those fleshly things which have been built into our lives: our experience, our education, our own human wisdom. We allow ourselves to be distracted by the things of this world and our eyes turn away from the Lord. Even though we know that He is the only important One, we still usually seek to live life our own way.

Yet, even humility is not a thing that comes from within us. The flesh is set against true humility because it makes us dependent and vulnerable. It is not natural for us to bow ourselves before another, at least not with whole hearts. What comes naturally is for us to bow down only when necessary, when faced with superior strength of some kind; even then, we reserve to ourselves a certain independence. Humility is not something we can simply call up from our own hearts.

So, we see that grace comes to the humble, but it is not in us to be humble. If we want to be humble, we must ask Him. Even our humility is a gift from Him. Humility in our hearts is a gift of His grace. Once again, the principle is obvious: He reaches down to us and provides all that we need, even the humility to bow in the first place.

Do you want to understand the truth about yourself? Then ask the Lord to show you why you depend on Him so much. Let Him show you your sin and your weakness. Let Him show you your need.

Then understand that grace is what God does for you. As you see your need, agree that the only provision comes from Him. Open your heart to His grace.

When God breathed that life into Adam, Adam would forever be dependent on the Lord for life. When Adam turned from the Lord in disobedience, what happened? The Scriptures teach us that Adam died and that we died in him.

> *Therefore, just as through one man sin entered the world, and death through sin, and thus death spread to all men, because all sinned.*
> *Romans 5:12*

Think about that for a moment. We must understand that there is no life in us and no good in us apart from Jesus. The only value we have is the fact that He is living His life in us. If that is true, then all our service for Him is of no value unless that service comes from Him. We cannot be good fathers and mothers or good husbands and wives unless He does that work through us. We cannot live under authority, we cannot love, we cannot even pray, unless He does the thing through us. It is nothing of us and everything of Him.

Establish an image of yourself bowed before Him and of Him reaching out to you in love because it is a good picture of grace. Whatever you need you must find in Him. He is your hope. He is your wisdom and your strength. He is your provision, your health, your love, your service. Everything that is offered to God through your life is offered by Him.

CALLING GRACE

Charles Spurgeon told a convicting story about the loss of the vessel called the "Central America."

> She was in a bad state, had sprung a leak, and was going down, and she therefore hoisted a signal of distress. A ship came close to her, the captain of which asked, through the trumpet, "What is amiss?"
>
> "We are in bad repair, and are going down; lie by till morning," was the answer.
>
> But the captain on board the rescue ship said, "Let me take your passengers on board now."
>
> "Lie by till morning," was the message which came back.
>
> Once again the captain cried, "You had better let me take your passengers on board now."
>
> "Lie by till morning," was the reply which sounded through the trumpet.
>
> About an hour and a half after, the lights were missing, and though no sound was heard, she and all on board had gone down to the fathomless abyss. [1]

Spurgeon used this as motivation for those in his audience to respond to the call of God on their lives immediately, without delay. He stressed the urgency of that call and the great loss to those who would ignore it.

As we look at the practical application of God's grace in the Christian life, it seems wise to consider why we are here in the first place. Why am I a Christian? Why are you a Christian? The answer is not as easy as it might seem.

In fact, theologians have debated that question for many centuries. Some suggest that we are Christians because we responded to the invitation to come to Jesus. Others claim that we are Christians because we were baptized as children. Still others say that we are Christians because we are part of some special group known as the "elect."

Aside from all the deep arguments, the Scripture simply makes it very clear that we are believers because God called us. Nearly all the debaters agree with this simple fact. Behind our choice or our association was a call from God. This idea of the call of God is a very important concept for us if we are to understand grace in our daily lives. In fact, we could say this is God's *Calling Grace*.

Remember our definition of grace? It is the Lord, in His majesty, holiness, wisdom, and strength reaching down to us in our helplessness to provide all our needs. The Lord is great and wonderful. We are helpless and needy. Grace is when He reaches out to us. Grace is what He gives to us. Grace is what He does in and through us.

Consider the Creator of the universe. He made it

all. Everything that exists has come from His command. He spoke the word, and out of nothingness came organization and substance. Nothing disobeyed Him, and nothing held Him back. From the most immense bodies of outer space to the tiniest parts of the atom, God created it all. Everything was in perfect obedience to Him. Everything was subject to His word.

Until He made humankind. Imagine the arrogance, the ingratitude of the man and the woman in the garden. There they stood, in the garden He had created, eating fruit He had made, in the bodies He had fashioned, and they turned their hearts away from Him.

With a word He could have destroyed them. He could have pushed them back into the dust of the earth and started again. He could have made them, forced them, to conform to His will. He could have done anything He wanted to them, but He decided simply to call.

The call of God is an act of His wonderful grace. He bowed Himself to us. In His majesty and glory, He bowed Himself to meet our need.

Theologians speak of two kinds of grace in connection with the call of God. The first is "common grace." This is grace shown to all humankind. This is the call Paul speaks of when he says:

> *For since the creation of the world His invisible attributes are clearly seen, being understood by the things that are made, even His eternal power and Godhead, so that they are without excuse.*

Romans 1:20

There is a call to every human being, no matter how wicked, no matter how far away from the nearest missionary, no matter what kind of childhood training he or she has had—a call to come to the Lord, a call clearly seen through the wonders of His creation. No one can escape this call, although anyone can reject it.

This "common grace" is what causes the rain to fall "on the just and the unjust." It accounts for the protection and provision given even to those who do not believe. It comes from His patience, His unwillingness that any should perish.

But we must understand that He is not required to give this "common grace" to anyone. The Lord reaches out in love to those who need Him, even before they know that they need Him. They don't understand that all provision and protection come from the Lord.

Those who are apart from the Lord in their thinking are never really out of His provision. When the day comes for them to stand before the Lord in judgment, they will see all the blessings they had from His hand, all the blessings they either ignored or for which they thanked others. They will see that His love for them was consistent and strong.

This is common grace: the great and mighty Lord God reaching down to the people of His creation to care for their needs despite their hopelessness and disobedience.

The other type of grace theologians speak of is "prevenient grace." Prevenient means ahead of time or grace beforehand. It refers to the special grace which called you and me to salvation.

Now, I doubt that there are many theological topics as controversial as the sovereignty of God in calling His people to Himself. Yet, the Scriptures are clear in asserting that no one comes to the Lord for salvation unless he or she has been called for that purpose by God's grace.

> *No one can come to Me unless the Father who sent Me draws him; and I will raise him up at the last day.*
> *John 6:44*
>
> *He chose us in Him before the foundation of the world, that we should be holy and without blame before Him in love.*
> *Ephesians 1:4*

He chose us before the foundation of the world! There are many explanations for the process of choosing that God used. Some suggest that He went through all potential human life and chose some to be saved and some to be condemned. They say that He chose to give a special, irresistible, call to those who would be saved. Others say that the Lord set up the way of salvation and allowed that only those who came to Him according to this way would be saved. Then He called everyone to Him through this way. Still others suggest that God has called all people to Himself and has accomplished their salvation apart from their personal response.

This discussion will continue until the day the Lord settles it forever. The simple truth of Scripture, that which is so important for you and for me, is that the Lord has chosen us.

> *"You did not choose Me, but I chose you and appointed you that you should go and bear fruit, and that your fruit should remain, that whatever you ask the Father in My name He may give you."*
> *John 15:16*

There was nothing special about us. He did not choose us because we were better than others. He did not choose us because we had sense enough to choose Him. He did not choose us because we were superior morally, intellectually, or in any other way. In fact, He says:

> *At that time you were without Christ, being aliens from the commonwealth of Israel and strangers from the covenants of promise, having no hope and without God in the world.*
> *Ephesians 2:12*

That was our state. Just the same as that of anyone else in the world. Yet, He chose us by His grace and called us by His grace unto Himself.

What He said to Israel about His choice of that nation still holds true for us:

> *For you are a holy people to the LORD your God; the LORD your God has chosen you to be a people for Himself, a special treasure above all the peoples on the face of the earth. The LORD did not set His*

love on you nor choose you because you were more in number than any other people, for you were the least of all peoples; but because the LORD loves you, and because He would keep the oath which He swore to your fathers, the LORD has brought you out with a mighty hand, and redeemed you from the house of bondage, from the hand of Pharaoh king of Egypt. Deuteronomy 7:6-8

It wasn't because of anything in us that He chose us, but it was because of His love.

So, what's the point? How is this knowledge valuable in our lives? I want to suggest that the knowledge of God's calling grace is important for two reasons.

First, it must keep us humble before the Lord. It is easy, after some time as a believer, to begin to think that we have somehow earned or deserved our place in the presence of the Lord. After all, we have tried hard to do what is right. We have tried to live in a different way than the world. It has been hard work and we have had to do things we didn't want to do. Sometimes we have had to hold back from doing things we really wanted to do. There is often a part of us that thinks we deserve some recognition, some benefit, for this extra effort. It is easy to pat ourselves on the back for coming to the Lord and for serving Him as much as we do.

Remember the parable of the Pharisee and the tax collector...

Also He spoke this parable to some who trusted in themselves that they were righteous, and despised others: "Two men went up to the temple to pray, one a Pharisee and the other a tax collector. The

Pharisee stood and prayed thus with himself, 'God,
I thank You that I am not like other men; extortion-
ers, unjust, adulterers, or even as this tax collector.
I fast twice a week; I give tithes of all that I possess.'
And the tax collector, standing afar off, would not
so much as raise his eyes to heaven, but beat his
breast, saying, 'God, be merciful to me a sinner!' I
tell you, this man went down to his house justi-
fied rather than the other; for everyone who exalts
himself will be humbled, and he who humbles him-
self will be exalted."
Luke 18:9-14

The only proper position before the Lord is on our knees. We must always remember that there was nothing in us that moved the heart of God to call us to Himself. We are humble before Him because we cannot show any reason for our place in the kingdom of Heaven except His grace, His love. We will always be dependent on Him.

The second difference this should make in our lives is that it should keep us humble before others. How can we look down on anyone when we realize that the only reason we have what we have is because of God's love? The only difference between the most wicked unbeliever and the most righteous among us is what the Lord has done. We have done nothing to make any difference.

Well, again, we have worked hard, haven't we? We have given up some of the pleasures of this world. We have worked toward building certain disciplines into our lives. We have struggled to make our lives better than others. How could we help but draw a distinction between ourselves and a murderer or a child-molester?

Yet, the Scripture is clear that there is no difference between the most corrupt molester and you and me, except for what Jesus has done in us. Apart from Him, without Him, we would be equal with the worst. When Paul and Barnabas went to Lystra, Paul healed a man who had never walked. The people saw the miracle and assumed that Paul and Barnabas were gods. They prepared to offer sacrifices to the evangelists.

> *But when the apostles Barnabas and Paul heard this, they tore their clothes and ran in among the multitude, crying out and saying, "Men, why are you doing these things? We also are men with the same nature as you, and preach to you that you should turn from these useless things to the living God, who made the heaven, the earth, the sea, and all things that are in them."*
> *Acts 14:14-15*

Are Christians better than others? Of course not. Jesus is better than others, better than anyone and anything, but you and I have value only because of Him. There is no place for us to think more highly of ourselves than we ought. If it were not for the grace of God in our lives, we would have the same lack of purpose and hope that unbelievers have. We are, as Paul says, no different *in ourselves* from those who remain lost.

When you and I think of ourselves, when we think

of those things that are considered our accomplishments or our virtues, we must remember the calling
grace of God in our lives. Were it not for His inter-
vention in our lives, however it is explained by the
scholars, we would be as lost as anyone. The state of
our lives would be hopeless.

Humility. That should be the continual state of
the Christian heart. Humble because of the knowledge of our complete and permanent dependence on
our Lord. Were it not for the grace of God, we would
still be in our sins, still without hope, still enemies of
God. The only reason we are saved is because He loved
us and called us to Himself. Praise the Lord!

****

[1] Northrup, Henry Davenport. Life and Works of Rev. Charles
H. Spurgeon. Memorial Publishing Co. 1892. p. 533.

SAVING GRACE

I came across a great little story from the *Sunday School Times* of years ago. It seems that there was a big evangelistic campaign in Kentucky in which the workers were using simple cards to share an important message. The cards were similar in size to a business card and read, "Get right with God." The cards were handed out all over the city.

The young boys who sold newspapers took a liking to the cards and put them on their caps. One day a strange bulldog came up to a group of the boys. They hadn't seen this dog before, but it was very friendly, even if it did have the appearance of being ferocious. The boys decided it would be good for the dog to have a card also, so they fastened one on its collar. Soon the dog went on its way and no one thought much more about it.

There was a certain man in this community whose reputation was such that many people had him on their prayer lists for the evangelistic campaign. That night, this man came out to the special meeting and, just as soon as the invitation was given, he nearly ran down to fall on his knees and give his life to Jesus. Everyone was amazed and excited.

Later, he explained what had happened. He had stayed home from work that day because he wasn't feeling well. In the afternoon he was trying to get some sleep when he was startled by this terrible growling and barking at his back door. At first, he tried to ignore the noise, but the animal was persistent, and he finally decided to get up from his nap to see what was happening. As he opened the back door of his home, the man was confronted by what he called "a fierce, ugly-looking bulldog," one he had never seen before in the neighborhood.

Of course, the man was somewhat frightened by the noise and the appearance of this dog, but when the dog saw him it stopped barking and started to wag its tail. Surprised by this sudden friendliness, the man sat down in a chair on his back porch and the dog came right up to him and put its head in his lap. There, staring the man in the face in a way he could not ignore, were the words, "Get right with God."

He told the listeners that if God was that interested in getting the message to him, he'd better give up. He had experienced the call of God.

In the last chapter, we considered the *calling grace* of our Lord. It is a call to salvation, to forgiveness of sin, to reconciliation. It is a call to a dramatic change. Let's consider that change.

We could tell so many stories of the amazing conversions of those who belong to Jesus. From the story of Paul to Augustine to Billy Sunday, there are thousands, perhaps millions, of amazing stories of great change. People who were deeply lost in sin found a new life in Jesus.

One young man seemed destined to a life of trouble. Rebellious and bold, he was jailed at the age of 16 for theft. He seemed incurably dishonest and lied even to his closest friends. He drank and partied and filled his life with sin. How could there be any hope for him?

Yet, at the age of 20, George Mueller found Jesus Christ. From that time on, a dramatic change was seen in his life. The rest of his life was spent serving the Lord he had mocked and ignored in his younger days. Today, his life is an example of faith and goodness for us.

Perhaps the best known and understood idea of grace is what we call, *Saving Grace*. In fact, most people will only think of saving grace when grace is mentioned. They have learned the Bible verses that are so well-known, and they have understood that there was no other way of salvation apart from the grace of God.

> *For by grace you have been saved through faith, and that not of yourselves; it is the gift of God, not of works, lest anyone should boast.*
> *Ephesians 2:8-9*

This message is true! There is no other way for you or for me to be saved. It is only God's grace that saves us, nothing of ourselves, just His loving grace.

But what does it mean to be saved? Just what did God in His grace do for us and to us in salvation? There are several important things that have changed in our lives because of God's saving grace. Before we look at these, it is important for us to realize and remember that none of these things would have happened except that He reached out to us in love.

Without worrying about any particular order, let me begin with the fact that we were guilty of breaking the law of God. The Scripture says:

> *For whoever shall keep the whole law, and yet stumble in one point, he is guilty of all.*
> *James 2:10*

Anyone who has broken one of the Ten Commandments, just one of God's laws, is as guilty as someone who has broken all of them. We were guilty of sin. If we were to stand in a courtroom, there would be only one plea for us—guilty.

Yet, because of the grace of God, we are justified.

> *And by Him everyone who believes is justified from all things from which you could not be justified by the law of Moses.*
> *Acts 13:39*

> *Being justified freely by His grace through the redemption that is in Christ Jesus...*
> *Romans 3:24*

That means that we are no longer guilty of sin. Yes, we did those things, but the sentence has been served. We are justified by the sacrifice of Jesus. He died so that we could live, and now we are no longer standing before the Lord in guilt.

In fact, we are forgiven. Before, we were fully accountable for our own sin.

> *The soul who sins shall die.*
> *Ezekiel 18:20*

We were accountable for every idle word.

> *But I say to you that for every idle word men may speak, they will give account of it in the day of judgment.*
> *Matthew 12:36*

Imagine being fully accountable for every wrong thing you have ever done! Who could bear that? We would stand before the Lord in the Day of Judgment and give account for every sin, no matter how small. What would we say?

Because of His grace, we don't have to say anything. We are no longer accountable for our past sins because our sins have been forgiven. There are no sins on our account because Jesus has forgiven us.

> *And you, being dead in your trespasses and the uncircumcision of your flesh, He has made alive together with Him, having forgiven you all trespasses.*
> *Colossians 2:13*

Because of our sins, we were separated from the Lord. There was nothing connecting us to Him. In fact, we were unable to enjoy His presence in our lives. Instead of the help and love that we feel from Him now, He could do nothing for us except allow us to go our own way and do our own things. He continually "gave us over" to the sinfulness of our hearts so that sin was our master. We belonged to the realm of sin. As He gave us over to sin, we were doomed to serve sin and to increase in wickedness, just as the Scripture says:

> *Therefore God also gave them up to uncleanness, in the lusts of their hearts, to dishonor their bodies among themselves.*
> *Romans 1:24*

But because He loved us, He, through His grace, has redeemed us. That means that He has purchased us. We were formerly slaves of sin, but now we belong to Him. He has redeemed us from the curse:

> *Christ has redeemed us from the curse of the law, having become a curse for us (for it is written, "Cursed is everyone who hangs on a tree").*
> *Galatians 3:13*

That's right, we were cursed and apart from the Lord, but He paid the price and bought us. He redeemed us with His own blood. He became cursed for us.

He died so that we could live. The Scripture is clear that those who are apart from Christ are dead in their sins. That's what we were, dead apart from Him. There was no hope for life in us because of our sin.

> *And you He made alive, who were dead in trespasses and sins.*

Ephesians 2:1

There was no life and no hope of life in us. But Jesus has, by His grace, made us to be alive. We were dead, in regard to righteousness and relationship with Him, and He gave us life. We are alive forevermore because of His grace.

> *For as in Adam all die, even so in Christ all shall be made alive.*
> *1 Corinthians 15:22*

> *Likewise you also, reckon yourselves to be dead indeed to sin, but alive to God in Christ Jesus our Lord.*
> *Romans 6:11*

We are now dead to the power of sin, dead to the punishment of sin, dead to the realm of sin, but alive in and through Jesus Christ. And we will live forever because of His grace.

Our lives were spent in darkness and wandering and would have continued that way except for His grace. Isaiah said it well:

> *Therefore justice is far from us, nor does righteousness overtake us; we look for light, but there is darkness! For brightness, but we walk in blackness!*
> *Isaiah 59:9*

But we no longer walk in darkness. Now, the light of Jesus Christ is within us.

> *Then Jesus spoke to them again, saying, "I am the*

> *light of the world. He who follows Me shall not walk in darkness, but have the light of life."*
> *John 8:12*

> *For you were once darkness, but now you are light in the Lord. Walk as children of light.*
> *Ephesians 5:8*

Not only darkness but trouble followed us all our days. There was no hope in those times of trouble because we were apart from the only source of help. Again, it is Isaiah who says:

> *Then they will look to the earth, and see trouble and darkness, gloom of anguish; and they will be driven into darkness.*
> *Isaiah 8:22*

Our Lord has given us His peace. His peace overcomes all our trouble if we trust in His grace.

> *Peace I leave with you, My peace I give to you; not as the world gives do I give to you. Let not your heart be troubled, neither let it be afraid.*
> *John 14:27*

I could go on for a long time with these amazing changes in our lives. He has done so much for us. Let me just point out a couple more.

Do you realize that we used to be enemies of God? Perhaps you didn't think of yourself as God's enemy, but the truth is that everyone who is a servant of evil is an enemy of God.

> *And you, who once were alienated and enemies in*

your mind by wicked works, yet now He has reconciled.
Colossians 1:21

For if when we were enemies we were reconciled to God through the death of His Son, much more, having been reconciled, we shall be saved by His life. Romans 5:10

According to the Scriptures we were saved while we were still enemies of the Lord. What are we now? We are the furthest thing from enemies, we are His children.

The Spirit Himself bears witness with our spirit that we are children of God, and if children, then heirs—heirs of God and joint heirs with Christ, if indeed we suffer with Him, that we may also be glorified together. Romans 8:16-17

That may be the most significant change of all. We who once were so far from God that we were His enemies have now become His children—by His grace.

So, you have been saved, if you have come to God through faith in Jesus. What you were, you are no longer. Salvation is not simply a rescue from justice, it is a dramatic, essential, change of your nature and your relationship with God. You have gone from being an enemy to being a child of God. You have gone from fear to peace. You have gone from darkness to light. You have gone from death to life.

These are facts of salvation. If you are saved, these things have been accomplished in you and for you by the grace of God in Jesus.

If you are saved... One of the benefits of living in a nation where the gospel has been so widely preached and our forefathers have embraced, for the most part, the faith of Jesus Christ, is that so many have heard and understood the gospel message of salvation. There is a corresponding concern to this. There are many people who assume that they are Christians simply because they have heard the message. They have attended church because it was the cultural thing to do. They have talked about Jesus and have believed in Him, but they have never trusted in His saving grace.

Maybe you have come to this place in this book, and you realize that the things presented in this chapter are not true of your life. Maybe you find them hard to believe. Maybe you are beginning to see that this saving grace has not been yours.

We learned that the call is from God. He is the One who reaches down to us in our need. Right now, He is reaching to you. He offers you forgiveness, full and free. He offers you a new life, one where He is actively leading. He offers you a new identity, one which can never be separated from Him.

Over the years I have used this illustration often: If someone comes to you and offers you a $50-dollar bill, how would you respond? It is a gift, with no strings attached. You don't have to do anything to get it, nor anything to keep it. Would you take it? Most of us would say that it would be foolish not to take it, right? But is the taking a "good work" on your part? Is there any credit of goodness to your account because you take the gift? No, you see it is not a matter of what you do; it is a matter of what you believe. If you believe that the gift is freely offered and that it has value for your life, then take it.

But understand what is being offered. If you have read this chapter, you know that salvation is not just "fire insurance." There is much more being offered to you. A new life and way of thinking, a new Master, is offered to you. It will make a difference, both in the future and today. Jesus is offering Himself to you and for you.

Saving grace can be yours today! Just open your heart to receive what is offered. Pray and tell the Lord that you wish to take what He wants to give to you. Tell Him that you want the whole "package"— the new life and all. Thank Him for offering it to you without cost.

Then believe! The whole message is true. He has done it all and He offers it to you. Yes, the story is amazing, but now it is your story!

CLEANSING GRACE

Among the legends of the days of King Arthur, perhaps the most popular is the story of the Holy Grail. According to the story, the Grail was the cup Jesus used at the Last Supper with His disciples. It came into the possession of Joseph of Arimathea, who used the cup to catch some of the blood of Jesus as He died on the cross. Later, the Grail was brought to England, supposedly to Glastonbury.

The tales of King Arthur, particularly the story of Percival, tell of the special powers of the Grail. The Grail would heal and purify anyone who drank from it. Those cleansing and healing powers, however, were available only to those who were pure in heart. To even look on the Grail without being pure in heart would bring instant punishment.

Consider the twisted story here. The Grail was holy because it held the blood of Jesus. It purified people. Only those who were pure in heart could receive the blessing of the Holy Grail. In other words, in order to be made pure you had to be pure in the first place.

Many people hold to this kind of thinking. They don't feel comfortable in the presence of Jesus because of something they have done, some sin that is in their past. They don't feel that they can come to Jesus because that sin has happened.

I had an intense discussion one day with another pastor who believed that people had to get their lives in shape, be pure in heart, before they could come to Jesus for salvation. He had spent his ministry telling people to be good and to do good things so they could be accepted by God.

How sad! The reason for the shed blood of Jesus is that we were unclean sinners in need of a Savior. If we must be cleansed before we can come to the Lord, we are in big trouble. We know that we cannot cleanse ourselves, that He is the only hope for us. How, then, could we ever be saved if we must be pure before we come to Him?

Well, of course, that is false teaching. It is so sad that many people still teach that way. What is even worse is that many Christians seem to have brought that idea into their Christian lives.

In this chapter I want to talk about what I will call *Cleansing Grace*. Our sins are washed away by the sacrifice of Jesus, and we are now cleansed and pure in Him.

Once again, so much of our understanding of the work of God in our lives centers around the time of our salvation. We are so moved and so dependent on that saving grace, that everything else seems to pale in contrast. I don't really think this is wrong; after all, nothing else in our lives would matter if we were not saved. However, for most of us there is a lot of earthly life to be lived after the moment of our salvation. If all there is to God's grace is what He did for us in that one action, then what do we do about the rest of our lives?

Of course, God's grace is for our whole lives. There is no point in our lives in which we are not completely dependent on His grace in order to be successful or to please Him.

This fact is important in relationship to the cleansing power of God in our lives. There are two burning questions in the lives of most believers, questions which are so significant that they can influence even the way we think about the Lord and His ways.

Here's the first: What about the sins I have done? Many Christians continue to be plagued by memories of things they did before they knew Jesus, before they were saved. For many there is a hesitation in their hearts and minds as they think of their own salvation. They know what the Bible teaches about salvation but—they know that their sins are forgiven but—there is this memory of a certain time or a certain offense, something that seems to be held over them threatening their eternal peace and joy.

It is hard for some to believe that God truly did forgive those offenses. They seem too great, too consequential. Yet, it is true! Those things are off your account. The penalty has been paid by the Lord Jesus Christ, and you can never be punished or held accountable for those actions again.

There is an important Biblical doctrine called "re-generation" which tells us what the cleansing grace of God has done in our lives. To be regenerated, in the Biblical sense, is to be "born again." This is what Jesus said must happen for salvation to be secured.

> *Jesus answered and said to him, "Most assuredly, I say to you, unless one is born again, he cannot see the kingdom of God."*
> *John 3:3*

As Jesus went on to explain, this regeneration is not simply a new physical beginning, a rebirth as we might think of it. This is a new person altogether, a being born of the Spirit. Peter explains further:

> *Having been born again, not of corruptible seed but incorruptible, through the word of God which lives and abides forever*
> *1 Peter 1:23*

Paul understood this and stated it as plainly as anyone could:

> *Therefore, if anyone is in Christ, he is a new creation; old things have passed away; behold, all things have become new.*
> *2 Corinthians 5:17*

This is the ultimate cleansing! Your sins were stuck to the old person, the person you used to be. Now you are a new person, and those sins are no longer a part of your life. No one can rightly remind you of the sins on your account because there are no sins on your account. Those things have not only been forgiven, they have, as the Scripture says, been removed from you "as far as the east is from the west." They are no longer yours.

Paul puts this in a very practical application as he writes to the church in Corinth.

> *Do you not know that the unrighteous will not inherit the kingdom of God? Do not be deceived. Neither fornicators, nor idolaters, nor adulterers, nor homosexuals, nor sodomites, nor thieves, nor covetous, nor drunkards, nor revilers, nor extortioners will inherit the kingdom of God. And such were some of you. But you were washed, but you were sanctified, but you were justified in the name of the Lord Jesus and by the Spirit of our God.*
> *1 Corinthians 6:9-11*

You <u>were</u> washed. You <u>were</u> recreated. Those sins are no longer on you. When the Lord looks at you, He does not remember those sins, no matter what they were.

So, if God can forget those sins, why can't we? Why do we still feel guilty? Let me offer a few brief reasons:

First, there is someone who doesn't want us to feel the peace and joy of the Lord. The evil one hates the Lord and His people and stands as our accuser day and night. Many times, when an old memory returns to your thoughts it is because the evil one wants to discourage you or move you to doubt the Lord and His love. In those times, cry out to the Lord for

His strength and thank Him for His cleansing grace. Thank the Lord for the new life He has given you and praise Him for what He has done in your life. This is the way to resist the lies and the fears brought by the evil one. When we praise the Lord for His truth, the prince of liars will flee.

Another reason we cannot forget is that there are often continuing consequences for our sins. The Bible never suggests that we will suddenly be free from all earthly consequences when we turn to the Lord. Sometimes that is given as a special gift from God, but usually not. If you signed for a loan you should not have gotten, you are still liable to repay that loan even if you repent. If you committed a crime, you may still have to suffer the earthly punishment for that crime. Some people see the consequences of their sin every day. No wonder they remember.

But listen: Just because you have continuing consequences does not mean that you are not forgiven! Those continuing consequences are things the Lord has allowed in your life for His purpose. They are reminders, perhaps, of how much He loves you.

How is that? Well, I would suggest that any reminder of the past sins should move us to give thanks to the Lord for His forgiveness. Consider those things memorial stones set in your life to give witness to what He has done. Use those reminders as motivation to praise Him all day long.

So, you see, you are a new creature in Christ. The person who did those things died with Jesus on the cross. Now you are someone new, someone different.

It is just as though you never did those things. Praise the Lord!

But there is another question that plagues the people of the Lord: What about the sins I still do? Do those sins affect my salvation? What if I do something terrible? What if I have a certain sin that I just can't seem to get rid of? How can those sins be washed away?

These questions have led believers to all kinds of interesting answers. Some have suggested that our sins break the bond between ourselves and the Lord, and we must be saved again and again. Others have gone so far as to assert that Christians cannot sin, that a real Christian will never sin again, and those who sin are simply not real Christians. Still others say that our sins after salvation can be forgiven if we confess them to the Lord and repent. If we don't, they suggest, then we are not forgiven.

Our family has been reading through the book of Matthew and we have been impressed with how Jesus would answer a question with a question. So, I want to answer these questions about our continuing sins with a question. What about suicide?

Let's say that a sincere believer becomes very depressed. It might be because of circumstances, it might be because of wrong thinking, or it might be because of chemical imbalances. Whatever the reason, the depression in this believer progresses to the point where the person takes his own life. The final act of this broken believer is self-murder.

Yes, I think that does happen sometimes. It

should never happen, just as no sin should happen in our lives. Yet, the evil one is persistent in his lies, and sometimes the consequences of our past actions do push us, and I believe it is possible for a believer to commit suicide.

But some ask: Will that person go to hell? Before you make your decision, remember that there is no room for sin in Heaven. No one with sin on his or her account will be in Heaven. It is either all or none. Either all sin is forgiven, or we are just as guilty as if none of our sins were forgiven. If the final action of a believer is an unrepented sin, will that person go to Hell?

How about the sincere believer who breaks the law by speeding and then dies in a car accident? Or how about the person who stuffs himself at the local buffet and dies of a heart attack? Or how about the person who has a stroke in the middle of a heated argument? Certainly, any of these could happen to a believer, right? Yet there is no opportunity for final repentance, no chance to go down the aisle one more time. Would that person spend eternity apart from the Lord?

No! The answer is no and here's why: the cleansing grace of the Lord continues throughout the earthly life of the believer. There is never any stain of sin on a believer.

We talked about the important doctrine of regeneration in the life of the believer, that wonderful ultimate cleansing that happens at the point of salvation. There is another important doctrine that enters in here, the doctrine of sanctification. If you study the idea of the cleansing grace of the Lord, you will notice that being washed and being sanctified are often referred to at the same time. To be sanctified means to be made holy or to be made acceptable—set apart—to God. This is part of His cleansing grace.

Years ago, near my wife's parents' home in Iowa, a railroad bridge was built to allow a main street across the city. Those who built the underpass knew that the walls would be a great place for delinquents to fill with graffiti. It was a large wall and the temptation would be strong. The decision was made to do something unusual. The walls were treated with some special material that would not allow paint to stick. To this day, some forty years or so later, there is no graffiti on those walls.

I did a little research on this and found that today there are several silicon-based products that do this. Apparently, the paint just doesn't stick. Even if the wall is sprayed, the rain will wash the paint off. Sounds like a good product to me!

This illustrates what the Lord has done in the life of the believer. Sin just doesn't stick! That isn't to suggest that we never sin, of course we do. Nor is it to suggest that our sin will have no consequences. We know better. But when it comes to our spiritual state, our eternal life, <u>there will never be sin on our account again</u>. Remember what Paul told the Corinthians?

> *And such were some of you. But you were washed, but you were sanctified, but you were justified in the name of the Lord Jesus and by the Spirit of our*

God.
1 Cor 6:11

We were washed, and today that cleansing is still ours. We are washed. We are sanctified. We are justified. Each of those is an eternal present. The past action of Jesus on the cross completed something in us. This is what we are now, because of the grace of the Lord. How much of the sin of our lives was forgiven in Christ? Was it just the 25% we committed before we came to Christ? After all, we have certainly sinned a lot more in the years since. How much has been forgiven? What did John write?

> *...the blood of Jesus Christ His Son cleanses us from all sin.*
> *1 John 1:7*

How much sin? All! All our sin has been washed away by the blood of Jesus. Not just the sin we committed before salvation but all our sin. That's the Word of God.

There are just a couple more things I want to be sure to say. First, this is not what has been called "sinless perfection." That is the teaching that true Christians will eventually reach the state of sinlessness in this life. I have not said that, nor do I believe it. Without question both experience and Scripture assert that believers will continue to transgress the laws of God. We will sin. We will also pay an earthly penalty for our sin. If we lie, we will find certain consequences in our lives from that lie. If we steal, we may be caught

DAVID ORRISON PHD

and judged just like any other person.

You see, we forget that there are many reasons not to sin. We don't have to sin because we are saved, and sin no longer controls our lives. We don't have to sin, and, therefore, we should not. But there are other reasons. The holiness of God should motivate His people not to sin. When we sin we give false testimony to His character. Our lives and this world are only made to work apart from sin. Sin will always cause negative consequences, even if those consequences are hard to see in the moment. The practice of sin is passed down to our children by our example, and they continue the priorities and values they have been taught. If we sin, they may sin in the same way or in other ways. Even more, sin hurts us and others. God would spare us the pain and suffering sin brings. There are many reasons for believers not to sin, serious reasons. We do not have to suggest that those who sin will lose their salvation.

Why does God continue to forgive our sins? We understand that He forgave us the first time because of His great love and our great need, but why should He continue year after year while we continue to disobey? Why doesn't He just give up and cast us away?

It may surprise you to learn that the Lord forgives our sins for Himself. We might think that forgiveness centers on us, but the truth is that it centers on Him. Listen to what He told Isaiah:

> *"I, even I, am He who blots out your transgressions for My own sake; and I will not remember your sins."*

Isaiah 43:25

He does it for His "own sake." He is holy and will not tolerate the presence of sin. He loved us and wanted us to be reconciled to Himself; but for us to be in His presence, we have to be clean. Not only does He wash away our sins at the time of salvation, but He continues to wash away our sins through sanctification for the rest of our earthly existence. Listen carefully: He keeps us clean because He wants us clean.

In other words, our salvation depends on His continuing cleansing grace. We can never be independent from the Lord again. We need His continuing work in our lives in every way.

So, when you go to bed tonight, give thanks to the Lord for His cleansing grace. Yes, there may be consequences for your sins in this life, but you can truly rest assured that there is no sin on your account with God. Yes, we should confess our sins, but not in order to stay saved. We confess our sins to be reminded of the great love of God and the great gift of His grace. John wrote it so beautifully:

> *My little children, these things I write to you, so that you may not sin. And if anyone sins, we have an Advocate with the Father, Jesus Christ the righteous.*
> *1 John 2:1*

Don't sin. It isn't worth it. It never does what you hope it will do. It always brings negative consequences. But if you do sin, turn back to Jesus and find the full and free forgiveness He has already given you. Trust in His cleansing grace and give Him thanks!

GROWING GRACE

The ancient Greeks had stories to explain so many things in life. We are told that their stories are about gods and goddesses and their interactions with humans, but I think most of them are more like parables, stories with which we can all connect. Some of these stories are thousands of years old yet are still told today.

One of those stories is about a king named Sisyphus. He was the king of a place called Ephyra, which later became known as Corinth. Four hundred years before Paul wrote his letter to the Corinthians, Plato wrote about Sisyphus—and the story was many centuries old by the time Plato got to it. Yet, we can all understand the point of the story.

Sisyphus was an evil king who managed to trick his way through life by being ruthless and smart. He didn't care who he betrayed or killed. Eventually, when he reached the afterlife, he was condemned to spend eternity pushing a large boulder up a hill. He would push that boulder with great effort all the way to the top only to have it roll back to the bottom again. Over and over, he spent his energy and his days on this never-ending job.

What is it at your house? Repairs, laundry, dishes, cleaning? No matter how much you do, there's always more. We all understand, don't we? We have all worked at jobs that seemed never-ending, where progress would never be found. I suspect that's why people have hobbies. Some like to garden, others like to build. Anything where you can see progress from your efforts. There is a human need for progress.

Imagine pushing that boulder up that hill, over and over, every day. Would it make a difference if you could get it just a tiny bit higher each time? Even if it still fell back down? It would, wouldn't it? If it could go an inch higher each day, there could be hope that one day you would reach the top and send it down the other side.

A century ago, a man named Emile Coue started something that would change the world, at least the worlds of his patients. He was a psychologist and a pharmacist. That might seem like an odd combination to us, but the pharmacist Coue realized that his patients were not getting better even with good medicine. He started studying the mind. In particular, he studied hypnosis and realized that the power of suggestion made a difference. So, he made a point of telling each person that the medicine was great and would work wonders. He discovered that people responded. In fact, to further test his theory, he would give the patients fake medicine, what we now call *placebos*. He would convince them that the medicine would work, and it did. Eventually, his simple words of affirmation became noticed by both the medical and the psychological professions.

You probably never heard of Emile Coue, but you have heard a little saying he invented:

> *"Every day in every way, I'm getting better and better."*

Not everyone appreciated Coue's work. The press and the medical community were very skeptical, just as people are skeptical of this kind of technique today. But even skeptics had to admit that people who used these words got better at a significant rate. Why? Because we want positive change in our lives. We want that little saying to be true in our lives. We want to see progress. We want to grow.

I remember a man who came to me years ago to tell me that he had reached the end of his Christian growth. I had been preaching on growing in Christ, but he felt he had grown as much as he ever would or would ever want to. I didn't quite know what to do with that.

Today, as I share the message of God's grace, it might sound like we no longer have growing to do. After all, Jesus did everything that was necessary for us to get to Heaven. He settled whatever was lacking in our accounts with God. He paid the price for our sin and selfishness. The Christian message is all about what Jesus has done for us and nothing about what we must do to earn our salvation. You and I, as we trust in Jesus, are as saved as we will ever be, as righteous as we will ever become, and as forgiven as we will ever need to be.

But we are still growing. The Christian life is supposed to be one of growth. We are called to grow. In fact, Peter said that those who don't grow will wander.

> *You therefore, beloved, since you know this beforehand, beware lest you also fall from your own steadfastness, being led away with the error of the wicked; but grow in the grace and knowledge of our Lord and Savior Jesus Christ. To Him be the glory both now and forever. Amen.*
> *2 Peter 3:17-18*

In other words, it isn't enough for us to stay the same, even if we use the word "steadfast." We can steadfastly become stagnant. Standing in the same place won't help to win the race.

What do you do with a new convert? If you share the truth about Jesus with someone and that person becomes a believer, what comes next? I remember people saying, even teaching, that you will want to keep the new believer away from old believers. The new believer will have energy and motivation for growing. The old believers, I was told, will do their best to stop that growth and make the convert as stagnant as they are. One of the reasons we see such an emphasis on new church plants is the desire of younger pastors to keep away from old believers. Oldy and moldy, they say.

Well, I understand this. I don't like it, but I understand it. I have met a lot of believers over the years, a lot who seem to think like the man who talked with me. They might have conquered an addiction or some bad behavior when they came to Jesus, but that's about it. They have heard the same sermons on the same texts for decades. New pastors come and go but the people stay the same.

I once had a man shake his finger at me and say, "Pastors leave, we stay." I knew what he meant. My time there was limited. But I would watch as people came into the church, sat in the same pew, folded their arms, and waited for the service to be done. They weren't about to learn anything because they barely listened. They thought they had heard it all. They stayed, but they didn't grow.

To grow in Christ means to have more confidence, more peace, more faith. It means we begin to leave behind the old ways and to enjoy the freedom and victory of the Christian life. It means to look less to the flesh and its habitual responses and look more to the Spirit who leads us to joy. It means to see others more the way Jesus sees them, to treat them with compassion and understanding as He did. It means to let more of this world fade away as we look to life without sin and darkness. More light, less confusion. Growth is something we all expected as we came to Jesus.

It may be that no one helped the old believers understand how to grow. If that's the case, it may also be only a matter of time before the new believers grow old. You see, no one grows in the Christian life by working hard. We don't grow by works; we grow by grace.

There are two ways the church has looked at grace through the centuries. One is to see grace, all grace, as a gift. Grace, as I have said many times, is what God does. He gives to us because He loves us. But a large portion of the church sees grace as ability, rather than gift. Grace, to them, is what God enables us to do.

Notice the difference because it is serious. On the one hand, grace as a gift says that you and I will not and cannot do anything for our salvation or our future hope. Jesus has done it all. On the other hand, grace as enablement says that it is still up to you and me to get to Heaven, but God will help us. The more we obey, the more He will enable us to do well. One is what Jesus does. The other is what you and I do. Paul would only see one of these as grace. The other he would call works or law.

Suppose you are called to cross a river. The river is wide and runs fast and deep. Along comes a man who says that he can get you across the river. That's great, you say, until you see that he has a hammer and some nails and a great pile of lumber. He gives you the hammer and says, "Well, there you go. Build yourself a bridge. If you need any advice or more tools, let me know. In fact, once you get the first part done, I will bring more lumber and nails." So, he keeps his word. You begin to build, and he provides the tools. But the river is wide and dangerous. It's hard work to build a bridge. And you have to eat and work your job and care for others at the same time. So, you don't get much built. After a while, he stops bringing lumber and nails because you haven't used what he brought last time.

That's a picture of grace as an ability. It looks a lot like work. It feels a lot like work. And, after a lot of effort and time, where do you find yourself? Still on the same side of the river. There is no progress. If it is up to you and me, there will be very little growth in our Christian lives.

Now, let's take that a step further. What if another man came to you in a boat and offered to take you across the river? His boat is strong, and he knows how to use it. All you must do is climb in and trust him. You will experience real progress as you sit and watch him row the boat. That's not work, that's a gift. That's grace.

Jesus told the people not to worry about their lives. He said to look at how God cares for the creatures of the air, providing their needs without daily chores. Then He told us how to grow. He said that worrying will not help us grow, neither will work. What will help us grow is receiving the gift of love, the grace of God.

> *And which of you by worrying can add one cubit to his stature? If you then are not able to do the least, why are you anxious for the rest? Consider the lilies, how they grow: they neither toil nor spin; and yet I say to you, even Solomon in all his glory was not arrayed like one of these.*
> *Luke 12:25-27*

"Consider the lilies." They don't have jobs. They don't worry. They don't labor day by day to grow. They absorb what God provides for them.

I can hear the objections. But we just don't understand their efforts. We can't see how they strain to reach water and nutrients. And the birds. They fly here and there looking for food. If they don't find it, they die. But Jesus made the point that you and I are not flowers or birds. We are persons made in the image of God, and He loves us. The point of the illustration is that we should be ready and willing to receive what God provides, then trust that He will provide all we need.

It is interesting that this illustration of growth is carried throughout the message of the Scriptures. Paul understood this. He wrote to the Ephesians that Jesus would build His church. He would grow the body that would be His bride.

> *And He Himself gave some to be apostles, some prophets, some evangelists, and some pastors and teachers, for the equipping of the saints for the work of ministry, for the edifying of the body of Christ, till we all come to the unity of the faith and of the knowledge of the Son of God, to a perfect man, to the measure of the stature of the fullness of Christ; that we should no longer be children, tossed to and fro and carried about with every wind of doctrine, by the trickery of men, in the cunning craftiness of deceitful plotting, but, speaking the truth in love, may grow up in all things into Him who is the head—Christ—from*

whom the whole body, joined and knit together by what every joint supplies, according to the effective working by which every part does its share, causes growth of the body for the edifying of itself in love.
Ephesians 4:11-16

Who will do all this? Jesus! He gave. He equipped. He edified. He joined and knit together the parts to make the whole. Jesus does this so the body will grow in love.

And for us as individuals, Paul says:

As you have therefore received Christ Jesus the Lord, so walk in Him, rooted and built up in Him and established in the faith, as you have been taught, abounding in it with thanksgiving.
Colossians 2:6-7

"As you have received Christ." How was that? As a gift of grace. By grace we have been saved. We did not receive Christ by working hard or doing more than others. We received Him as He came to us. In faith, we opened our hearts to what He wanted to give.

So, Paul says: in the same way, walk in Him. Find that progress and growth you desire. You are "rooted" in Him and have been "built up" in Him and are "established in the faith" by Him, so move forward in the same way. That means trusting in what He has and will give.

Let me suggest two words that describe Christian growth: *abiding* and *receiving*. Jesus gave us the ultimate illustration in the story of the vine and the vinedresser.

> *"I am the true vine, and My Father is the vine-dresser. Every branch in Me that does not bear fruit He takes away; and every branch that bears fruit He prunes, that it may bear more fruit. You are already clean because of the word which I have spoken to you. Abide in Me, and I in you. As the branch cannot bear fruit of itself, unless it abides in the vine, neither can you, unless you abide in Me. I am the vine, you are the branches. He who abides in Me, and I in him, bears much fruit; for without Me you can do nothing. If anyone does not abide in Me, he is cast out as a branch and is withered; and they gather them and throw them into the fire, and they are burned. If you abide in Me, and My words abide in you, you will ask what you desire, and it shall be done for you. By this My Father is glorified, that you bear much fruit; so you will be My disciples.*
> *John 15:1-8*

Set aside for now the whole question of what happens to branches that are cut off or pruned. Ask only one question: What is expected of us? If Jesus is the Vine and the Father is the Vinedresser or Gardener and we are the branches, then what are we supposed to do? The only thing expected of us is to abide.

Abiding does not mean becoming stagnant or passive. It does not suggest a lack of growth. Instead, it shows us real growth. We are to rest in the One who provides all we need for growing and producing fruit. Jesus will do the work of providing. The Father will adapt our circumstances and us so that we can receive what Jesus gives to us. All we are asked to do is receive.

By now you should be asking what this looks like in practice. What does it mean to abide and receive? What should I do and what should I expect?

If the Spirit reveals an area in your life that needs growth, look to Jesus to provide that growth. Let's say that you have someone in your life who is hard to love. Look to Jesus for the love you need. Ask Him, trust Him, and receive what He gives. Let your growth be in His hands. If you want to worry less about money or relationships or the future, look to Jesus. Ask Him to grow peace in your heart and joy in your daily life.

When the disciples saw their own lack of faith, they looked to Jesus and asked, "Increase our faith." Did He do that? Of course. These followers became people of great strength because they trusted in Jesus for everything in their lives. They taught others to do the same. Through personal trials and painful struggles, they found Jesus to be enough. They grew because they asked for growth, even in faith.

We are called to grow, but Peter makes it clear what the goal of our growth is to be:

> *But grow in the grace and knowledge of our Lord and Savior Jesus Christ. To Him be the glory both now and forever. Amen.*
> *2 Peter 3:18*

We do not seek to grow stronger so we can do more on our own. We seek to grow in the "grace and knowledge" of Jesus. In other words, to receive more and more from Him. As we do that, the things of this world, the worries and compromises, will begin to fall away. We will see and enjoy more of the "things that are above." We will become more of who we are.

CONQUERING GRACE

The story is told of a woman who lived in the Bronx and had her apartment broken into many times. She tried putting locks on her door, but the burglar was quite intelligent. He seemed to be adept at picking locks. Instead of getting new locks on her door, the woman put more locks on it. Soon she had seven locks on her door, and she had to call the locksmith for another. However, just hours after the locksmith put on the eighth lock, she called to say that it had been picked again.

Suddenly, the locksmith had an inspiration. He suggested that the woman only lock four of the locks at a time. That way the burglar would be locking as many as he was opening and would be frustrated.

He didn't hear from the woman for several days. Finally, she called with great excitement in her voice. It worked, she told him. Every time she came home, she found that the four locks she had locked were unlocked, but the four she had left unlocked were now locked.

Harry Houdini was the greatest escape artist of all time. He could get out of anything, jail cells, boxes under water, straitjackets, anything. But one time he was foiled. It was a little country jail cell in the British Isles. He was placed into the cell and left alone. In an instant, he was on that lock working feverishly. He tried all his tricks, used all his hidden tools, anything he could think of, but nothing worked. He could not trip that lock. He worked faster and faster until he was almost completely exhausted, but still the lock remained unchanged. Finally, he collapsed and fell against the door. Amazingly, the door opened. The lock had never been locked.

How many of our battles have already been fought and won? How many of the victories we seek are already ours? How many of the problems we seek to conquer have already been conquered? How many?

All of them!

There is no question that the Christian life is a life of battles. We have enemies, powerful enemies, who want to discourage us and mislead us from the service and grace of the Lord. Those enemies are always around us, it seems, and they truly are strong.

Of course, we are not talking about people. People might be the tools of our enemies, but, as the verse says, we are not battling people:

> *For we do not wrestle against flesh and blood, but against principalities, against powers, against the rulers of the darkness of this age, against spiritual hosts of wickedness in the heavenly places.*
> *Ephesians 6:12*

Our enemies are spiritual enemies. You have often heard that Christians have three main enemies; the world, the flesh and the Devil. Each of these is already defeated, already overcome by God's *Conquering Grace*.

As we study Scripture, we see over and over a variety of principles. These principles can be carefully applied to areas of our lives not specifically addressed by the Scriptures. Of course, we have to be careful because this can also be misused. The context of Scripture will reveal if we can do this.

The principle of fighting enemies illustrates what I mean. How should God's people fight their enemies? The Scripture is clear that whenever God's people put their full trust in Him, He will give them the victory. It will be very clear that they had no real part of the victory, that it was His grace.

Look at the story of David and Goliath. There was an uneven match! Yet, David overcame the giant because his trust was in the Lord. It was the Lord's victory. The reason David could walk out onto the field that day in confidence was because the Lord had already delivered the enemy into his hands.

Remember the story of Jehoshaphat in 2 Chronicles 20? This is one of our favorite stories. One day, Jehoshaphat gets the word that there is a large number ("a great multitude") of soldiers on the edge of his territory and they are coming to destroy Judah. There isn't time to get the armies together. There isn't time to make alliances to help with the battle. There isn't time to do anything—except pray.

While many thousands of enemy soldiers are camped nearly at the doorstep, Jehoshaphat calls the people together for a great fast. They pray and seek the Lord. I especially like the prayer Jehoshaphat offered on that day.

> *Then Jehoshaphat stood in the assembly of Judah and Jerusalem, in the house of the LORD, before the new court, and said:*
> *"O LORD God of our fathers, are You not God in heaven, and do You not rule over all the kingdoms of the nations, and in Your hand is there not power and might, so that no one is able to withstand You? Are You not our God, who drove out the inhabitants of this land before Your people Israel, and gave it to the descendants of Abraham Your friend forever?*
> *And they dwell in it, and have built You a sanctuary in it for Your name, saying, 'If disaster comes upon us; sword, judgment, pestilence, or famine; we will stand before this temple and in Your presence (for Your name is in this temple), and cry out to You in our affliction, and You will hear and save.' And now, here are the people of Ammon, Moab, and Mount Seir; whom You would not let Israel invade when they came out of the land of Egypt, but they turned from them and did not destroy them; here they are, rewarding us by coming to throw us out of Your possession which You have given us to inherit. O our God, will You not judge them? For we have no power against this great multitude that is coming against us; nor do we know what to do, but our eyes are upon You."*
> *2 Chronicles 20:5-12*

"We don't know what to do, but our eyes are on you." How many times could you have prayed that prayer? Well, the Lord loves His people. He heard their cries for help. He saw that they were focused on Him. Then He told them something wonderful:

> *And he said, "Listen, all you of Judah and you inhabitants of Jerusalem, and you, King Jehoshaphat! Thus says the LORD to you: 'Do not be afraid nor dismayed because of this great multitude, for the battle is not yours, but God's. Tomorrow go down against them. They will surely come up by the Ascent of Ziz, and you will find them at the end of the brook before the Wilderness of Jeruel. You will not need to fight in this battle. Position yourselves, stand still and see the salvation of the LORD, who is with you, O Judah and Jerusalem! Do not fear or be dismayed; tomorrow go out against them, for the LORD is with you."*
> *2 Chronicles 20:15-17*

The battle was the Lord's. The people went to the battle singing the praises of the Lord. When they reached the battlefield, they found that their work was already done. The enemy was destroyed. God's conquering grace had been at work on their behalf.

Grace is when the Almighty, wise, and majestic Lord reaches down to us in our hopeless conditions and situations and meets our needs. There was nothing the people of Judah could have done that day to win the battle. They needed the Lord. When they turned to Him in faith, His grace was truly sufficient.

What are the battles you face today? Let's look at those three major enemies of the believer. Can we ever hope to overcome the evil one? There is no doubt in my mind that the evil one is strong. He is also very intelligent. He is more intelligent than we are, and he is also stronger than we are. So, what hope do we have when he is after us?

Yet, John writes particularly to the young men and reminds them that they have overcome the evil one.

> *I write to you, fathers, because you have known Him who is from the beginning. I write to you, young men, because you have overcome the wicked one. I write to you, little children, because you have known the Father.*
> *I have written to you, fathers, because you have known Him who is from the beginning.*
> *I have written to you, young men, because you are strong, and the word of God abides in you, and you have overcome the wicked one.*
> *1 John 2:13-14*

How could they do that? We understand that Satan is an angel of the Lord. The Scripture tells of one angel destroying the entire army of Israel's enemy. How could we, as weak and helpless people, stand against the evil one? We don't have to, do we? Satan might be stronger than we are, but he is not stronger than our Lord. Later in his letter, John speaks of overcoming the forces of the evil one:

> *You are of God, little children, and have overcome*

*them, because He who is in you is greater than he
who is in the world.*
1 John 4:4

The one in us is greater than the one in the world.
Who is in the world? Satan! Who is in us? Jesus! Jesus
is greater than Satan and has overcome him. The conquering grace of the Lord Jesus Christ is active in
our lives because He is active in our lives. When we
belong to Him and submit to Him, we are invulner-
able. Satan cannot touch us apart from the love of the
Lord.

Does the evil one attack the people of God? Oh
yes! His purpose is to discourage and distract. But we
can overcome him just like the Scripture says.

*And they overcame him by the blood of the Lamb
and by the word of their testimony, and they did
not love their lives to the death.*
Revelation 12:11

In other words, the evil one is overcome because
of what Jesus has done and is doing in us. When we are
His, the evil one has no victory in us. You might hear
talk of great spiritual warfare, but you must remember that Satan is a defeated enemy, defeated by the
power of the Lord. Can he influence your life? Yes, but
only by his lies. He has no power over you, no authority in your life. You belong to Jesus, and your Lord is
more powerful than the evil one.

What about the world? We live in a world that is
increasingly corrupt and deceitful. How can we over-

come the world and its influence in our lives? Jesus said it very clearly:

> *"These things I have spoken to you, that in Me you may have peace. In the world you will have tribu-lation; but be of good cheer, I have overcome the world."*
> *John 16:33*

He has overcome the world. Why is that good news for us? Because it means that the world has no power over us. We belong to Jesus Christ, and He is greater than the world. No matter how evil this world becomes, we do not have to be afraid because our Lord has overcome the world. Through Him we also conquer the world.

> *For whatever is born of God overcomes the world. And this is the victory that has overcome the world; our faith. Who is he who overcomes the world, but he who believes that Jesus is the Son of God?*
> *1 John 5:4-5*

So, we don't have to worry about the devil or the world. Most of us have understood that already. We might not always feel the victory over these enemies, but we know it and can remember it at times. But what about the third enemy?

Of the three enemies we face, the flesh certainly seems to be the hardest to overcome. The struggle is so subtle and so daily. This seems to be the one enemy we will never overcome in this life. All our bad habits, all our wrong attitudes, all our weaknesses are bound up with our flesh.

We need the reminder and the hope of the fact that Jesus Christ has already conquered our flesh. Just like with every other enemy we face, the One who overcomes the flesh in us is Jesus. Through faith, we accept the victory He has died to give to us.

Now, I understand that you might not feel victorious over the flesh, so let's look at what the Word says to us. First, in what I consider the ultimate statement on grace, Paul tells us that our daily lives are to be lived by faith.

> *I have been crucified with Christ; it is no longer I who live, but Christ lives in me; and the life which I now live in the flesh I live by faith in the Son of God, who loved me and gave Himself for me.*
> *Galatians 2:20*

We receive God's grace through faith. Even though we live in the flesh daily, the flesh does not have to have victory over us. You see, we need to separate the fact that we are with and in the flesh every day from the fact that we are free from the flesh and victorious over it.

Consider what happens when you swim. Water is a hostile environment for any air breather. Water could be said to be a serious enemy of life. Yet, when you swim, you are surrounded by that enemy and not overcome by it. You conquer the water when you swim.

In much the same way, we live in the realm of the

flesh all the time, but we are not slaves of the flesh. Instead, just like the water, the flesh becomes our slave as we keep our eyes on the Lord Jesus Christ. Through faith we can live victoriously even while we live in the flesh.

The victory we enjoy as believers has come to us by God's promise. The promise of God is dependable. In Galatians 4, Paul is talking about the life under the law in contrast to the life under grace. He reminds us of the two sons of Abraham:

> *But he who was of the bondwoman was born according to the flesh, and he of the freewoman through promise, Galatians 4:23*

Paul says that this is a symbol of law and grace or the flesh and the spirit. True freedom is the result of the gift, the promise of God. We are not in bondage to the flesh because we are born through the promise to the Spirit. Therefore, we are victorious over the flesh. This is God's conquering grace at work for us.

We are also victorious over the flesh because the flesh has been put to death. Consider what Paul says in Galatians 5:

> *And those who are Christ's have crucified the flesh with its passions and desires.*
> *Galatians 5:24*

The Scripture says that anyone who comes to Jesus Christ dies. The old man is dead, but his effect not gone. He influences our lives by the memories and habits he built, but he has no power over us. We don't have to live the old way according to the flesh. We don't have to bow to those old habits and passions. Instead, we are now under the control of the Spirit, and we live no longer under the flesh.

Finally, let's make this very clear. We know that sin separates us from our Lord. We know that there is no sin in the kingdom of God. We know that nothing corrupt is allowed in His presence. We also know that there is no good thing in the flesh. That's what Paul admits to himself and to us in Romans 7:

> For I know that in me (that is, in my flesh) nothing good dwells; for to will is present with me, but how to perform what is good I do not find.
> Romans 7:18

If there is no good thing in the flesh and if the flesh is corrupt, then the flesh should keep us apart from the Lord, right? Wrong—but only because the Lord Jesus Christ has had victory over the flesh in us. The flesh has already been conquered.

> Who shall separate us from the love of Christ? Shall tribulation, or distress, or persecution, or famine, or nakedness, or peril, or sword? As it is written: "For Your sake we are killed all day long; We are accounted as sheep for the slaughter." Yet in all these things we are more than conquerors through Him who loved us.
> For I am persuaded that neither death nor life, nor angels nor principalities nor powers, nor things present nor things to come, nor height nor depth, nor any other created thing, shall be able to separ-

> *ate us from the love of God which is in Christ Jesus*
> *our Lord. Romans 8:35-39*

We are more than conquerors. Nothing will keep us from the Lord, not even our own flesh. Nothing is that powerful. There is no enemy, not even the most familiar, that has not been conquered by the conquering grace of the Lord Jesus Christ.

This is the fact of Scripture. I understand that this might not feel true because of the daily walk and daily struggle of the Christian life, but it is true, nonetheless. When you and I face the enemies who come after us, we must remember the truth. They might seem strong. They might seem invincible, but they are not. We are victorious. We have no enemy who can stand against us. All enemies, even death itself, are under the feet of our Lord. He is the Conqueror.

When you find yourself in battle, whether it be battle with an old habit or battle over fear or whatever, cry out to the Conqueror. Look to Jesus. Sing His praises. Consider His power and wisdom and love. Pray and focus your heart on Him. The victory is already yours through His conquering grace.

OBEYING GRACE

Over her long history, England has often been at war. In one story, the Australians, out of loyalty to the British during a time of war, wanted to do whatever they could to help. The word came back to them that the mother country needed ships. They asked for ships to be built. Ships would have made the difference.

Well, the Australians didn't know what to do. They didn't build ships. They didn't have shipyards. They decided that they would raise food for the armies and the people at home instead. They went to work with a passion and raised a huge amount of grain. This they sent to the water's edge so that it would be ready when the ships from England came. But the ships never came.

Instead, the mice got into the grain and disease began to spread around the city. Many people were infected, and lives were destroyed. All the while, the leaders in England were asking for more ships.

Not only military leaders struggle against problems with obedience. Medical doctors say that one of the most serious and pervasive problems they face is the patient who will not follow orders. Some patients feel that if one pill is good, two will be better, often putting themselves at risk and negating the good the medicine was supposed to do. Others begin to feel better and abandon their treatments too soon. One study indicated that up to 90% of patients cheat on diets, continue to smoke, don't return for check-ups, or stop their medication too early.

Obedience should be a simple thing. All we have to do is what we are told. Of course, there may be times when what we are told to do isn't right, but those times are in the minority. They never happen when God is the authority.

Certainly, believers should have no trouble obeying our Lord, right? After all, we understand that He is wise and kind and that He has our best interests in His heart. When He tells us not to do something, it should be easy for us to stop it or never to start it. When He tells us that we should do something, we should easily obey with joyful enthusiasm. Right?

Well, it doesn't usually seem to work that way. Simple obedience isn't very simple. In fact, simple obedience can be one of the most difficult things for us to do.

Now, I am not talking about the kind of obedience we would find in ourselves if the Lord spoke to us out of thin air. If you or I were walking on the sidewalk and the Lord suddenly started speaking to us out of a bright light no one else could see, we would probably obey His command. We might test it to be sure it was Him, but if we knew it was the Lord, we would do it, no matter what it was.

We appreciate the faith of Abraham who was told to sacrifice his only son, or Noah who was told to build a big boat, or the shepherds who left their sheep to find the baby Jesus. We appreciate that kind of faith but, in the background, we remember that they did these things because the Lord spoke to them. We think that if the Lord spoke to us in the same way we wouldn't have any trouble obeying either.

We shake our heads at Adam and Eve. They had only one rule. There was plenty of other food to eat. We could have obeyed the direct word of God, especially if there was only one rule. Or so we think.

I don't know about that. What I do know is that the Lord has already spoken to us about a lot of things and we do have trouble obeying, even some of the simple ones. It would be very difficult to find a believer who sincerely walks, moment by moment, in obedience to the will of the Lord. Instead, most of us try to obey, want to obey, but fail all too often.

Yet, obedience is important. Some teachers and believers have downplayed the idea of obedience. They have taken the idea of God's grace to mean that they have no responsibility and no standards by which they should live. Anything goes, they suggest, because of the wonderful grace of God. It is certainly possible to be a believer and still have a rebellious heart. There is no question that some of those who teach this come from that perspective. They are already set against the idea of standards and control and obedience, so they embrace a doctrine which allows them to make decisions according to their own desires.

There are also those who simply have given up. Obedience is impossible in their minds. They are not particularly rebellious, but they just can't keep up the constant fight. This false perspective of grace gives them a sense of freedom from obedience.

The only problem, of course, is that this is clearly against the will of God for His people. He desires obedience. In fact, He desires obedience in such a way that He has promised blessings for those who obey and punishment for those who do not. Listen to what the Scriptures say you will receive:

> ...the blessing, if you obey the commandments of the LORD your God which I command you today; and the curse, if you do not obey the commandments of the LORD your God, but turn aside from the way which I command you today, to go after other gods which you have not known.
> Deuteronomy 11:27-28

> "I call heaven and earth as witnesses today against you, that I have set before you life and death, blessing and cursing; therefore choose life, that both you and your descendants may live; that you may love the LORD your God, that you may obey His voice, and that you may cling to Him, for He is your life and the length of your days; and that you may dwell in the land which the LORD swore to your fathers, to Abraham, Isaac, and Jacob, to give them."
> Deuteronomy 30:19-20

If they obey and serve Him, they shall spend their days in prosperity, and their years in pleasures. But if they do not obey, they shall perish by the sword, and they shall die without knowledge.
Job 36:11-12

Now someone will say, "Sure, but that's the law and we are no longer under the law. Those words don't have any bearing on our lives." Is it only the law that calls us to obedience? I don't think so. Listen to what was written for those under the realm of grace. We should be...

...casting down arguments and every high thing that exalts itself against the knowledge of God, bringing every thought into captivity to the obedience of Christ. 2 Cor 10:5

Therefore gird up the loins of your mind, be sober, and rest your hope fully upon the grace that is to be brought to you at the revelation of Jesus Christ; as obedient children, not conforming yourselves to the former lusts, as in your ignorance; but as He who called you is holy, you also be holy in all your conduct 1 Pet 1:13-15

Not only is obedience expected of the people of the Lord under grace, but perfect obedience. We are to bring every thought into obedience. We are to be holy in our conduct. That's a far greater challenge than what was urged under the law.

Clearly the benefits of obedience are great, and the negative consequences of disobedience are also great. We must obey the Word of the Lord. We must obey the Holy Spirit's conviction in our hearts. How can there be any other choice for someone who belongs to Jesus Christ?

Obedience should be easy when we look at it from this perspective. What motivation could be so strong that we would turn our backs on God's blessings and embrace the negative consequences? Why would we, who have been saved by His supreme sacrifice of love, disobey Him?

Yet, of course, we do disobey. That's why we need what I am calling *Obeying Grace*. This is important: we have seen that we have been called by His initiative in His *Calling Grace*. We have been saved by His work in His *Saving Grace*. We have been cleansed by His power through His *Cleansing Grace*. We already have the victory over all things through His *Conquering Grace*. All of these are His activity of grace on our behalf. All of these are what He has done.

Wouldn't it be foolish of us to suggest that obedience is now up to us? This is the question Paul asks the Galatians as he chastises them for their "Christian life by works" ideas.

> *O foolish Galatians! Who has bewitched you that you should not obey the truth, before whose eyes Jesus Christ was clearly portrayed among you as crucified? This only I want to learn from you: Did you receive the Spirit by the works of the law, or by the hearing of faith? Are you so foolish? Having begun in the Spirit, are you now being made perfect by the flesh? Galatians 3:1-3*

"Are you now being made perfect by the flesh?" In other words, "Can you suddenly walk in obedience through the flesh?" No, of course not. The only hope for obedience in our lives is through the grace/life of the Lord Jesus Christ in us.

The more we understand the truth of the Scriptures, the more we realize that only disobedience comes from the flesh. The reason we find it hard to obey our Lord is because of the continuing influence of the flesh in our lives. There is no hope that we will ever walk in obedience if it is up to us.

That's where obeying grace comes in. Now, I suspect that this is may be the most difficult aspect of grace to apply in our lives. This is our daily walk. This is the realm of those bad habits, those wrong attitudes, those hurtful decisions we so often have. This is where we live. At this point we can no longer talk about theory. We can no longer be content to think that this grace business is wonderful. Now, if this is right, we should be able to see the way for our lives to be different. This is where the rubber hits the road.

There are always those who want formulas and equations, a way for the analytical mind to understand. There does seem to be a formula for obedience. Of course, I must be careful with this. I am not suggesting that there are five easy steps to obedience or that there is any mathematical formula for success, but that there are three building blocks which lay the foundation for obedience in our lives. They are taught throughout the Scripture, and I think you will find them helpful.

You see, the word for *obey* in both the Old and New Testaments stems from the word which means "to hear." The concept of obedience is tied directly to the concept of hearing in both Hebrew and Greek. In fact, this is true in some aspects of English as well. In older English, such as the King James Version, people were called to "hearken" to the voice of the Lord. That meant both that they should hear and obey.

To hear is to obey. Those are the words of a servant to a master. The story is told of a missionary who wanted to find just the right word to translate the concept of obedience into the tribal language. He searched and struggled but couldn't seem to find what he needed. As he walked to his home in the village one day, he whistled for his dog which came running at full speed to be with his master. The native who was with him noticed this and commented in the tribal language that the dog was "all ear." That was the word the translator needed. To obey was to be "all ear."

So, the first foundation block of obedience is to hear the word of the master. That doesn't always happen in our lives. Jesus suggested that certain people were "dull of hearing." They were so intent on listening to the things of this world—the applause of men, the tinkle of gold coin, the threats of the enemy— that they no longer heard the Lord's voice. How could they obey His voice when they couldn't even hear it?

Perhaps by now you are beginning to understand that God wants to give you the things He asks of you.

If you desire to hear His voice, particularly with all the distractions of this life, you must ask Him. Simply ask Him to open your ears and your heart to His voice.

Yet, just hearing the word of the Master isn't enough. Another foundation block is needed. When Jesus went among the people, they heard His words, but most of them did not understand. He wanted them to understand.

> *When He had called the multitude to Himself, He said to them, "Hear and understand..."*
> *Matthew 15:10*

Hear and understand. That was the key. In an earlier chapter we considered the parable of the sower who scattered seed on four types of ground. Only one kind of ground produced fruit. That ground, Jesus explained, represented a different kind of people.

> *"But he who received seed on the good ground is he who hears the word and understands it, who indeed bears fruit and produces: some a hundredfold, some sixty, some thirty."*
> *Matthew 13:23*

The one who hears and understands will produce good fruit. That makes sense, doesn't it? How could you obey a voice you did not understand? Not only do you have to know what is being said, you must know what it means.

Now, when it comes to the Lord's word, that doesn't mean that you must understand why He says something; just that you must understand what He wants you to do. If He says, "Do not steal," you simply should not steal.

So, far so good. The Lord has taken the initiative of revealing Himself and His will to us. I suppose we could call that His "revealing grace." What I mean is that we do not have to search for Him, He has reached out to us. His voice, through His Word and through the testimony of the Spirit within us, can be heard—if we listen.

The Lord has also given us the ability to understand His Word through His Holy Spirit. There are mysteries and deep doctrines, but the things we need to do or to avoid are made clear and understandable for those who have the Spirit at work in them. When we accept the life of Jesus Christ, the Holy Spirit begins His "understanding grace" in our lives. The gospel and the things of the Lord are great mysteries to those who are unbelievers. It should not be so with us.

Yes, there are times when we hear, and we do not understand. There are also those times when we hear and understand and still disobey. Why? What else is there? Jesus knew what the problem was. He knew the truth about us. He knew why we would still disobey.

There were two different occasions on which Jesus miraculously provided food for the multitudes from a small offering of loaves and fish. It has always been interesting to me that the disciples asked the same questions the second time as they did the first. When Jesus told them to feed the people, they didn't see how that was possible. The first time we could excuse, I suppose, because they didn't understand who Jesus was. Yet, even after the miracle, they still didn't understand. There was a reason...

> *For they had not understood about the loaves, because their heart was hardened.*
> *Mark 6:52*

Their hearts were hardened. That was the reason they did not understand. Later, when they still questioned at the second opportunity, Jesus brought it home to them.

> *But Jesus, being aware of it, said to them, "Why do you reason because you have no bread? Do you not yet perceive nor understand? Is your heart still hardened? Mark 8:17*

He knew that the real problem, even with His closest disciples, was the state of their heart. If their hearts were hardened against His word, they would not obey. They would be uncooperative.

Obedience depends on hearing and on understanding, but it will never happen as long as the heart is hardened. So, it is obviously worth our while to try to understand what it means to have a "hardened heart."

The most famous story about a hardened heart is the story of Pharaoh. As Moses proclaimed, by word and action, more and more of the power and glory of God, Pharaoh's heart became increasingly hard. From that story, we usually get the idea that a "hardened heart" is one set against the Lord. There are two problems with that. First, it seems harsh to suggest that the hearts of the disciples were set against the Lord. They loved Jesus, and they gave up much of their lives to follow Him. Certainly, they would not agree that they were set against Him in their hearts.

The second concern with this view is that there are passages where we are told that the Lord was the One who hardened Pharaoh's heart.

> But the LORD hardened Pharaoh's heart, and he did not let the children of Israel go.
> Exodus 10:20

Theologians are rightly concerned about any time when we might suggest that the Lord is the Author of sin, or that He pushes individuals into unbelief. So, what do we do with this? If we are to avoid the hardened heart in ourselves, we need to understand what it means.

Perhaps the understanding of this difficult doctrine can be illustrated by the hardening of an egg in boiling water. Consider that the boiling water represents the corrupt environment of a sinful world or of the life that is used to sin. All the stresses and temptations and troubles of the broken world serve to harden the heart. It is not so much that the heart is hardened against the Lord but simply that it becomes hardened or calloused in its approach to life.

When you go through life, you encounter certain obstacles. In order to overcome those obstacles, you develop habits, methods, ways of thinking that help you move toward what you consider to be success. For example, a child who is abused might learn to duck or to hide, and some type of avoidance technique may continue into adulthood. He has developed an approach to life that has served him reasonably well. Others might suggest that it is dysfunctional, but it works for him, and he often doesn't realize what he does.

What have most of us learned through our lives? We have learned that success comes either from working harder or from being smarter than others. We have learned that the only ones we can count on are ourselves. We have learned that it is somehow wrong or dangerous to depend on someone else. This has become our way of thinking, our approach to life.

We are in that boiling water of our own perspectives, supported by our experience of life and the values of the world around us.

Now, notice this: The only thing a person does to harden an egg is leave it in the boiling water. The hardening process is natural. The longer the egg is in the boiling water, the harder it will get.

I am convinced that this illustrates the idea of the hardened heart. It isn't necessarily that we intend to be set against the Lord, but that the natural process of life in the flesh hardens our hearts increasingly. Pharaoh's heart was hardened by the process of his own unbelief. When God allowed him to continue in that unbelief, the natural direction was for him to become more hardened.

We would think that the disciples would be different. They looked to Jesus in faith. Perhaps their faith was small, but it was faith. Yet, their thinking continued on the same general track as it did before they met Jesus. They saw the awesomeness of the task, rather than the awesomeness of the Master. When He asked them to feed the multitude, even the second time, they didn't think about His ability to do the miracle, but their own inability to do such a thing.

So, a "hardened" heart is one that continues the same path of thought, the same flesh-centered perspective. A hardened heart will not obey the voice of the Lord because its perspective is wrong. If the Lord tells you that it is time to move from your job, your hardened heart might think of all kinds of reasons why that would be a bad idea. What would you do for money? What about the years of tenure you have? Where would you go, and what would you do? It isn't that these are wrong thoughts or sinful questions, but that they all must be balanced against the truth of God's great love for you and your family and His ability to provide.

Ok, so how do you deal with a hardened heart? You begin to think differently. You remember that the work belongs to the Lord. You remember that the power and provision always come from Him. In other words, you look to His real activity in our world and in your life, and you recognize that grace is His work in and for you. The way of thinking is the key to obeying.

And do not be conformed to this world, but be

transformed by the renewing of your mind, that
you may prove what is that good and acceptable
and perfect will of God.
Romans 12:2

Was Jesus asking His disciples to give bread and fish to all the people of the multitude—from themselves? Of course not! They were to act in obedient faith and know that He was fully able to accomplish the thing He desired. He wanted the people fed, and He was going to feed them. Obedience simply meant moving in the direction of His activity.

You see, obedience is not about getting results. So, often we are bound up by our unbelief, our hardness of heart, because we focus on the result. We can't see how we could accomplish that thing, so we don't move in that direction. But the results are in the hand of the Lord. Remember: He does His work! Our part is to move the way He is moving.

Do you want to obey the Lord? I am going to assume that every reader of this book would answer that affirmatively. If you want to obey the Lord, ask Him for *obeying grace*. Understand that to mean that you will trust Him for the results and that you will simply begin to move in the direction He is moving. You will allow Him to begin to change your thinking, your perspective on life.

He will do this. He will transform your thinking as He shows you His ability. You will learn to trust Him more, and you will learn to look to Him first.

PRAYING GRACE

In evangelical circles there is a great deal of talk about the Christian roots of our nation. It is true, and important to remember, that many of the early leaders of our country were Christians. They loved the Bible, and they believed its words. When they designed a system of law and government, they looked to the Lord's teachings for wisdom.

Perhaps one part of this story that is often forgotten is that this country was founded on prayer. The personal practice of prayer was a significant part of the early success of our nation.

You have heard of the amazing group of believers called the Moravians. Their prayers may well be responsible for the Christian nature of this country. In the beginning of their movement in Herrnhut, they set apart two groups dedicated to prayer. Twenty-four men were in one group and twenty-four women in the other. Their covenant was to pray around the clock for the kingdom and glory of God. That prayer lasted over a hundred years!

Out of that prayer came the ministry of John and Charles Wesley. Their preaching and teaching changed hearts on both sides of the ocean. John Wesley prayed at least two hours every day and was said to be in the habit of not going one full hour without prayer. There is a letter by someone who didn't seem to like Wesley's company for this reason. He felt that Wesley could never relax because it was Wesley's custom to break up every visit that lasted an hour by taking some time out for prayer.

The Moravians prayed. The Wesleys prayed. Even the political leaders in those days prayed. George Washington prayed seriously. His custom was to rise at 4:00 every morning and spend time with the Lord. He prayed often and always kneeling. In fact, at one point a stranger came to the rooms where the legislature was working and wondered how he could identify Mr. Washington. He was told to watch as they gathered for prayer. "Washington will be the one kneeling."

Any study of grace must be surrounded by prayer. Any new understanding of grace will probably be preceded by prayer. Any new application of grace in the Christian life will be accompanied by prayer. Asking and receiving are the foundation stones of practical grace.

We have seen the need to come to the Lord for the provision of all our needs, even to ask for His grace. When the evil one accuses us, we should pray. When we find the temptation to disobey, we should pray. When we find doubt in our hearts, we should pray. Yet, most believers, if honest, would admit to far less prayer than they feel they should have in their lives.

You see, prayer is easier to talk about than to do for some reason. In fact, prayer, or lack of it, is one of the leading causes of guilt in the Christian life. We believe in the importance of prayer, but we just don't pray. We have such a great need to pray, but we find ourselves just too busy. We tell people that we will pray for them, but then we forget. God sometimes seems like a stranger to us, and prayer is often just another burden.

Why does prayer seem like a burden? Why does it seem impossible to spend an hour in prayer? Why do we forget to pray, when we know how important it is in our lives?

There are two reasons, at least, why prayer becomes a burden. The first is the activity of the evil one against prayer. Something I have experienced consistently in my ministry are those interruptions during times of important prayer. Some of you will attest to this. Just when you sit down with your seeking friend and begin to pray with that person—what happens? Sure, the telephone rings, the dog bites one of the kids, someone is at the door, something, anything, to distract from that prayer. The evil one will seek to pull hearts out of prayer whenever he can.

After a while we learn to pray about praying. That is, we ask the Lord to surround our prayer time with His protection. We ask that there would be no interruptions other than those He would consider important for us. We ask that He bind any evil force that might seek to distract from this precious time. In other words, we pray about praying.

Now, the second reason prayer becomes a burden is probably more serious and more widespread. Prayer becomes a burden for the same reason witnessing is a burden or giving is a burden or reading the Word is a burden. The burdens of the Christian life come from only one place—the flesh. Whatever is done in the flesh becomes a burden.

Can we pray in the flesh? Yes, and I would suggest that we usually pray in the flesh. In fact, the flesh is the real reason for our difficulty and our lack of success in prayer. You may remember that the Bible speaks of several reasons for unanswered prayer. In fact, because of some of these, we are told that God will not hear our prayers. Holding onto iniquity, wrong relations between husband and wife, lack of forgiveness in our hearts; these are all things of the flesh. When we focus on ourselves, in other words, we cannot focus on our Lord, and our prayers are worthless. Prayers in the flesh are worthless.

So, again, we need to pray about praying. If prayer is truly a thing of the Spirit, then we need the work of the Spirit in our lives in order to pray. Prayer is a burden, a frustration, a waste of time, when it comes from our flesh; but, when it comes from the Spirit, prayer is that powerful connection to our Lord that makes all the difference.

That connection is what we want in our lives. We want nothing to hinder our prayers. We want to receive all the grace of God that He desires to give us. If prayer is what we should do, then we need to learn to pray.

One day when Jesus was deep in prayer, his disciples watched with amazement. I think His practice of prayer must have made a serious impression on them. His prayers are mentioned often in the gospels. They realized that there was power and blessing for Him in His prayer times. So, that day they decided to ask Him to teach them to pray.

This should also be our prayer. "Lord, teach me to pray." First, we must understand that prayer is not a burden. Reject any thought that prayer is anything less than a great blessing, a treasure of the Christian life. Otherwise, we won't even pray about praying. Accept by faith that prayer is better than it might seem and that the worst prayer in the Spirit is more worthwhile than the greatest fleshly counterfeit.

So, what is prayer? We usually say that prayer is talking to God. Unfortunately, that's all it is for most people, even for most believers. And what is the purpose of prayer? To get God to do something, right? Again, that is usually the purpose of prayer in our lives. We come to the Lord when we want something, and prayer is the tool we use to tell Him what we want. This shallow and self-centered idea hides the fact that here is so much more to prayer.

I want to suggest two radical changes in the way we look at prayer. The first has to do with the purpose of prayer, and the second has to do with the true nature of prayer. The purpose of prayer is not quite what we have been trained to think.

I like what Ole Hallesby said in his classic book on prayer:

"To pray is to let Jesus come into our hearts."[2]

The purpose of prayer, then, is to open ourselves to Him. As we pray, we assume, if we are praying according to the Spirit, the posture of receiving grace: on our knees before the wise, wonderful, and loving God. Our desire, as we seek His grace, is to be fully yielded to Him, to have nothing stand between us and our Lord, to hold nothing back from Him or His touch.

Please don't misunderstand! I know that there are people out there suggesting that we must assume certain physical postures in order to achieve certain results in prayer. Consider what I am saying to be a "posture of the heart." We bow our hearts in humility and submission, whether we bend our knees or not.

We remember, when we pray in the Spirit, that it doesn't matter what we say. What matters is what He says. It doesn't matter what we do, it matters what He does. He is the center of our thinking and of our feeling. As we bow before Him, we see ourselves in our need, and we open ourselves to His grace and mercy.

> *Likewise the Spirit also helps in our weaknesses. For we do not know what we should pray for as we ought, but the Spirit Himself makes intercession for us with groanings which cannot be uttered.*
> *Romans 8:26*

The purpose of prayer is to release from our focus the world, the flesh, and the enemy and to set our hearts on the Lord. Imagine the joy of being fully in His presence!

This is the opening of the prayer Jesus taught His disciples.

> *"Our Father, which art in Heaven, hallowed be thy Name. Thy kingdom come, thy will be done on earth as it is in Heaven."*

All of that is focused on the Lord. Jesus is telling His disciples that their first thought should be to submit themselves to the Lord.

Now, that's the purpose of prayer. The nature of prayer is always praise. What I mean to say is that prayer is always praise, all true prayer is praise. Let's think about that. We know what it means to praise God. We tell Him the little that we understand of His greatness. We acknowledge His glory, His beauty, His holiness, His wisdom; all the wonders of God that keep us in awe of Him.

We also praise God when we thank Him. We acknowledge our need for His gifts, and we acknowledge His great generosity. When we thank Him, we humble ourselves before Him and remember both our need and His love. To properly see ourselves in relation to Him and to honor Him by submission and humility—that is highest praise.

But have you ever considered that even your petitions, when offered through the Spirit, could be praise? When we bow in prayer to express our need, we are reminding ourselves and confessing before Him that we need His grace. When our need drives us to our knees before Him, He is lifted up in our hearts just as certainly as if we were singing songs of great praise.

So, my suggestion is that all true prayer is praise to God. Right prayer will lift the Lord higher in our hearts and minds and will move us to submit even more of ourselves to Him. Right prayer, as Hallesby said, "is to let Jesus into our hearts."

When we pray then, we must remember that all prayer is praise. Ask yourself, before you pray, how your prayer praises Him. How does your request praise the Lord? Are you coming to Him for something with yourself in mind or with Him in mind? Are you coming to Him with your praise in your heart or His?

There are two things we must remember. The first sounds simple but could radically change the way you and I pray. We must never tell God what to do. That puts Him in the servant position and us in the position of the authority. When we come to Him and say, in effect, do this or do that—even if we say please —we are asking Him to serve us. That isn't praise to Him.

Instead, we must acknowledge before Him our need. Let me say it this way: <u>Never tell God what to do. Tell Him what you need.</u> Do you see the difference? When we come to Him with our needs, we are in the position of the needy servant and He is in His proper place as the loving and powerful Master. We are bowing before Him seeking His grace.

That brings me to the final, but perhaps most important, point. We must always pray in Jesus' name. That doesn't mean that we must always say the

words, "in Jesus' name," although that might be helpful to remind us of how we come to God. The particular words we say are not the point, not some kind of
magic formula. Instead, our hearts should know just
how we do come to God.

The only way you and I can come to the Father is
through Jesus. There is no access to the Father for us
apart from the Son. We bow before the Father; carrying as our banner the name of Jesus.

> *And whatever you ask in My name, that I will
> do, that the Father may be glorified in the Son. If
> you ask anything in My name, I will do it.*
> *John 14:13*

You see, when Jesus says that we come "in His
name," He means that we belong to Him.

We must abide—find our life—in Jesus. When we
come to the Father, we must fully acknowledge our
total dependence on Jesus. We cannot come in our
own names because that would lead us to pride. Instead, we are humble before the Father. We remember
that it is only because of His amazing gift of love that
we can come to Him at all.

It gets us back to that posture of receiving grace.
Even proper prayer is submission to Him. Even praying grace comes from Him. We can do nothing of ourselves. We must come to Him even to pray.

Then, when we are fully yielded to the Lord, humbled before His presence, the Scripture says:

> *Likewise the Spirit also helps in our weaknesses.*

For we do not know what we should pray for as we ought, but the Spirit Himself makes intercession for us with groanings which cannot be uttered. Romans 8:26

This is praying grace in its fullness. We are no longer the leaders, but we are observers of the wonders of the great God. He gives the prayer and hears the prayer and answers the prayer, and in all of it He is glorified.

When you pray, and we are to pray "without ceasing," remember that prayer is a great blessing, an opportunity to praise God in every way. Come to Him in humility and brokenness and reveal what you know of your need. Come to Him in the name of Jesus, as one who bears the very life of the Son. Then see if He hears you. He will, and His answers will amaze you. He will receive all the praise and glory, and you will receive the blessings when you have found praying grace.

****

[2] Hallesby, Ole. Prayer. Augsburg Publishing House. 1931. p. 4.

WAITING GRACE

I recently ran across some correspondence my father had with a company about a replacement part for one of their products. He wrote a letter to the company asking about the part. They wrote back to him asking some questions about the product. He wrote again telling them the information. They wrote to him telling him the price and availability of the part. He wrote back asking them to send the part and included a check to cover the costs. Finally, the part arrived in the mail. (I only had part of the correspondence, so I am guessing at some of this.)

Now, if everything worked well, and both the company and my father responded quickly, a minimum of five weeks must have passed between the first letter and the arrival of the part. If not, it could have taken a few months. Imagine waiting maybe two or three months to get the part you need for the broken appliance. How would a customer react today?

Today, we would order the part online and expect it to arrive in two days. At most, we would call the company, discuss our options and place the order over the phone. Then we would still expect the part in a couple of days. We would not expect to wait long today. And we wouldn't even wait that long, if we could find someone who had the part locally.

And, of course, my father's correspondence would have seemed fast to my great-great-grandfather. He drove a stagecoach at one point in his life. He may well have carried mail to people who had waited many months for an answer to their question.

We hate to wait, don't we? It doesn't really matter how long we must wait. Our ancestors probably complained about waiting months or years to hear from family or government. We grumble about waiting days. If we are standing in line or sitting at a stoplight, we complain about minutes. There's something about waiting we really don't like.

Yet, waiting is part of our lives. Someone has calculated that the average person spends approximately six months of their life waiting in lines. We spend thirteen days on hold with customer service each year. (I know it seems a lot longer.) The average commuter, a person who must drive to work, spends thirty-eight hours a year held up in traffic. It may be much longer for some of you. We have to wait a lot.

But, of course, it's more than that. Young people wait to grow up, wait for their birthdays, wait for school to be done. Older people wait at the doctor's office, wait for the kids to visit, and wait for the commercial to end. We wait to hear back from a job interview or a business decision.

And we wait for the Lord to work. To find the right

person to marry. To be healed from our pain. To get that promotion. To find the right house. We wait for a word from God to move on a decision. We wait for the Lord to provide something we need. We wait to be reunited with those who have gone before us. If we add in all that waiting, we could certainly say that we spend most of our lives waiting.

And, still, we don't particularly like it. No matter how often someone tells us that God's timing is right or that He knows what is best for us, we still find waiting hard and unpleasant.

So, we tend to be suckers for the fast-track gimmicks. "Lose seven pounds in seven days!" "Write your novel in a month." "Learn Spanish in a week." We even think we can get God to move faster with a gimmick. Pray this certain prayer, and God will do what you want now. Do this certain act of service to get this benefit. Give and get more.

But I have noticed that God often is not in a hurry when I am in a hurry. Not only does He not answer all my questions, He just doesn't do things when I want Him to do them. In fact, when I think I need for Him to do them. Instead, I wait.

While in Egypt, the Hebrews waited for a deliverer to lead them out of slavery. In the days of the kings, the faithful Israelites waited for a good king to restore the kingdom. They waited for the Messiah to come. The believers waited for a new emperor in Rome or whatever country they lived in, someone who would treat them right. Then, along with all of us, they waited for the coming of Jesus to take us home. Millions of believers have waited thousands of years for the last days to come. Waiting on the Lord is part of the Bible story.

So, okay, we don't like waiting, but we have to do a lot of it. You might be waiting for me to get to the point. But I must ask a question first: Why don't we like waiting? What's so bad about it? We understand that there's a difference between waiting a whole minute for the light to change or two minutes for the water to boil and waiting for generations to see the coming of the Lord. Yet, they are much the same. Waiting for the light to turn green is an indication that life doesn't revolve around us. Nor can we control the people in the other cars. They might not notice the light turn because they are on the phone, talking with a passenger, or just distracted. So, we react against our lack of control.

And isn't that the real problem with waiting? Our lack of control? If there is one thing that regularly reminds us that we are not in control, it's waiting. Our desire for instant gratification is really a desire for control. We want it when we want it, whether it's moving through traffic or physical healing. Our fantasy would be to snap our fingers or speak a word and get whatever we want right away. People would do what we want when we want it. The weather would change according to our desires. Life would work by our plans and in our timing.

The evidence of our desire for control lies in our anger as we must wait. We call it frustration, but it's just anger. It is a characteristic of our flesh to bristle when it doesn't get what it wants. And, yes, sometimes we even get angry with God. Waiting for healing. Waiting for justice. Waiting for recognition. Waiting for love. Sometimes waiting turns us bitter.

In English, the word "wait" is very old and simply means to watch. In Hebrew and Greek, the words are much the same. They mean to look for. Waiting is an active verb, even though we feel frustratingly passive as we do it. When you wait for your number to be called at the DMV, you watch and listen. When you sit at the traffic light, you watch for the red to turn to green. When you need money, you might watch the mail for the check to come. When you pray, you look to the Lord to meet your need.

Like the dog that watches the hand of the master, or the birds that wait in the trees for the feeder to be refilled, we wait for the hand of our Master to move on our behalf. And when we look to Him, we are blessed.

Waiting is a blessing under grace. I know that sounds strange. I know that doesn't even sound right. It doesn't feel like a blessing. Yet, if I were to ask you if you wanted to be stronger, you would almost certainly agree. The Scripture promises that those who wait become stronger.

> *But those who wait on the LORD shall renew their strength; they shall mount up with wings like eagles, they shall run and not be weary, they shall walk and not faint.*
> *Isaiah 40:31*

If I were to ask you if you wanted to be blessed with many good things, you would agree again.

> *For evildoers shall be cut off; but those who wait on the LORD, they shall inherit the earth.*
> *Psalm 37:9*

God blesses those who wait on Him. Good things come to us as we wait on the Lord. But notice that this isn't just sitting and moping and grumbling. Waiting on the Lord is looking to Him. Those who look to Him will be blessed.

Although we may no longer know the tunes, the words of the Book of Psalms continue to touch our hearts. For 3000 years, these "songs of Israel" have reflected the struggles of our hearts. David, the king of Israel, wrote most of the psalms out of his own feelings. They are honest questions and statements of a man who loved the Lord but suffered so much. And we all connect with him when we read passages like this:

> *Save me, O God! For the waters have come up to*
> *my neck. I sink in deep mire, where there is no*
> *standing; I have come into deep waters, where the*
> *floods overflow me. I am weary with my crying; my*
> *throat is dry; my eyes fail while I wait for my God.*
> *Psalm 69:1-3*

"My eyes fail while I wait for my God." Wow. When there are no more tears to flow, no more voice to cry, no more words to say. When we have no energy left even to worry or complain. What are we supposed to do then? When we have nothing left, where do we go? For most of us, that's when we begin to truly look to the Lord.

As touching as the psalms are, and as much as we identify with the feelings they state, none of us would read them if they ended in the pain. We don't need someone to remind us of our sadness or emptiness. We need hope, and hope comes from the Lord. The psalms minister to us because David reveals the word God gives to him in the midst of his heartache. That word from our loving Lord encourages us as well.

Psalm 69, quoted above, is a particularly poignant song. David speaks of those who want to destroy him, of friends and family who have turned against him, and how he has become a joke to the people who used to admire him. He feels overwhelmed by the oppression, like he is being sucked deeper into a pit filled with muck and water. He knows no way of escape and feels himself giving up. He grieves for what he has lost. He is angry against those who brought this on him. And he looks to his Lord.

This is a messianic psalm, a song that presaged the suffering of Jesus, that is quoted at the cross.

> *They also gave me gall for my food, and for my thirst they gave me vinegar to drink.*
> *Psalm 69:21*

It reminds us that the Lord Himself suffered

and waited for deliverance. He who knew the truth looked to the Father for help. And even Jesus found peace as He waited for His answer.

Almost all the psalms that reveal the struggling of David's heart end with a strong word of assurance. That assurance is even stronger when it comes out of suffering. This psalm ends like this:

> *But I am poor and sorrowful; Let Your salvation, O God, set me up on high. I will praise the name of God with a song, and will magnify Him with thanksgiving. This also shall please the LORD better than an ox or bull, which has horns and hooves. The humble shall see this and be glad; and you who seek God, your hearts shall live. For the LORD hears the poor, and does not despise His prisoners. Let heaven and earth praise Him, the seas and everything that moves in them. For God will save Zion and build the cities of Judah, that they may dwell there and possess it. Also, the descendants of His servants shall inherit it, and those who love His name shall dwell in it.*
> *Psalm 69:29-36*

When David looked to the Lord, he saw only love and promise. The pain will not last forever. The struggle will end. The promised deliverance will come. Whatever happens, the love of God is sure. However the present trouble ends, the love of God does not waver.

You see, when David looked to the Lord, he did not see a system or a doctrine or a tradition. He saw a Person. David didn't fall back to platitudes and mem-

DAVID ORRISON PHD

orized words; he fell back into the hands of the living and loving God. David may have been the most grace-filled believer of the Old Testament. The reason he could always find hope was because he looked to a real Person. He knew the Lord.

The message of grace must always present the person of Jesus, the Messiah of Israel, the Lord God Almighty who loves us so much. Neither our goodness nor our faith will get us through long times of waiting. The love and constancy of the Lord is what gets us to the end. Grace is about a Person.

How do you and I find the grace to wait? By looking to Jesus. All the promises for us will be fulfilled in His time. Our hope is in our Lord, not in the things we have done or the associations we have kept. He may move slowly or differently from what we expect, but He moves with wisdom and power for our good. If we look to Him, we find that He is our strength. For one more day, we find the strength and peace we need, and then for another and another after that.

A word that should never be disconnected from waiting is "hope." When we despair, like Job did in his suffering and loss, it feels as though even hope is lost. He thought he should just die and be done with all of it.

> *"What strength do I have, that I should hope? And what is my end, that I should prolong my life?*
> *Job 6:11*

But Job did know the Lord. His words seem so negative, so defensive, that we sometimes miss his hope.

> *For I know that my Redeemer lives, and He shall stand at last on the earth; and after my skin is destroyed, this I know, that in my flesh I shall see God, Whom I shall see for myself, and my eyes shall behold, and not another. How my heart yearns within me!*
> *Job 19:25-27*

When Job looked to the Lord, he found his hope and his strength. When David looked to the Lord, he saw his hope and strength. We have a champion, great and mighty, who loves us. We have a deliverer, a healer, a friend. When we wait, even in times of great struggle, the Person of our Lord is our strength.

This is what David knew. Yes, he forgot sometimes, especially as he faced challenges, but the Lord would reach out and call him back, and David would find his strength renewed. In the course of one psalm, we read David's despair and the Lord's reassurance. David wanted those who would sing his songs to look to the Lord. And, for 3000 years, we have found our strength in Him.

> *I wait for the LORD, my soul waits, and in His word I do hope. My soul waits for the Lord more than those who watch for the morning. Yes, more than those who watch for the morning. O Israel, hope in the LORD; for with the LORD there is mercy, and with Him is abundant redemption.*
> *Psalm 130:5-7*

The pain and anger that comes from waiting is

simply an indication that our eyes are off the person of Jesus. When we look to Him and see His love and grace, our strength is renewed.

There will be a day without pain and suffering, when the waiting is over. In part, that may come in this life. In fullness, that is ready for us in glory. By grace, we can experience the strength and hope Jesus offers to us in this life. David tells us that the secret of his ability to climb out of despair was seeing the truth.

> *I would have lost heart, unless I had believed that I would see the goodness of the LORD in the land of the living. Wait on the LORD; be of good courage, and He shall strengthen your heart; wait, I say, on the LORD!*
> *Psalm 27:13-14*

We will not wait forever. Our Hope stands like a mighty warrior to do battle for us, like a good friend at our bed of suffering, and like a great King who offers us all good things. Under grace, we know Him. Under grace, we trust in His love. Under grace, we find our strength in Him—even as we wait.

That day of rejoicing will come. Our God does win the war. Those who have waited on Him, who have looked to Him, will share in His victory.

> *And it will be said in that day: "Behold, this is our God; we have waited for Him, and He will save us. This is the LORD; we have waited for Him; we will be glad and rejoice in His salvation."*
> *Isaiah 25:9*

GIVING GRACE

Little children know the story of Zacchaeus because he had to climb a tree to see Jesus. As the crowds pressed around Jesus, Zacchaeus was too short to see the Teacher. Little children know what it means to be short and to try to see interesting things when tall adults are in the way. So, Zacchaeus climbed a tree. We read the story in Luke 19.

Now, this is one of those stories where we wish we could know more. Jesus had captured Zacchaeus' heart, as well as his interest. When Jesus walked the path where Zacchaeus was in the tree, He looked up and called out to the man. He said, "Zacchaeus, make haste and come down, for today I must stay at your house." If this was a surprise to Zacchaeus, it was surely a pleasant one. Zacchaeus "joyfully" welcomed Jesus into his home and, we understand, into his life.

If all we learn about Zacchaeus is that he was short, we certainly miss the point of the story. Zacchaeus was a tax collector, a profession hated by the Jews. He was a Jew who worked for the Romans. Tax collectors had the reputation of being hard and unfair. They demanded payment from those who had little or nothing and, according to the stories, inflated their demands for their personal gain. The people saw tax collectors as compromised, greedy, and cruel.

So, when Jesus said that he would go to Zacchaeus' house, they criticized the Teacher. They could not understand why Jesus would go to the home of such a man, a sinner, they said. In fact, the text says, "they all complained." No one understood.

But when Zacchaeus stood up in his house and told Jesus that his heart had been changed, Jesus rejoiced. Zacchaeus said that he would give half of his riches to the poor. In the second verse of the story we are told that Zacchaeus was not just a tax collector, but a "chief tax collector." That meant he oversaw other collectors and probably received a portion of what they collected. Perhaps one of the earliest "pyramid schemes." In any case, we are told bluntly that Zacchaeus was rich.

He would give half of his wealth to the poor and return four-fold to anyone whom he had cheated. Here was a genuine change of heart, a new heart in a man touched by Jesus. And Jesus rejoiced to see that "salvation has come" to Zacchaeus and his house. The purpose of His coming, Jesus said, was to find people like Zacchaeus and save them.

A couple of chapters later in Luke, in chapter 21, Jesus arrived in Jerusalem and sat with His disciples in the Temple. There were chests positioned in the Temple courts where people could put their offerings. Jesus sat down, perhaps tired from teaching, and watched the people putting their offerings into the chests. The picture we get is that the rich people drew attention to themselves as they gave their gifts. But, as Jesus watched, a poor widow slipped near the chest and deposited two mites. A mite was the English term for the smallest coin in circulation at the time. The Greek word was "lepton." Jesus said the two coins were all she had and that they were worth more than all the rest put together.

This story is, of course, well-known by preachers and used to encourage people in giving. They say that we should give according to our means, that the rich should give more than the poor, but all should give. To find further support for this idea, they reach back to Old Covenant law and bring out the tithe. The tithe was a percentage-based giving structure, they say. Giving the tenth part, 10%, of what you make equalizes rich and poor, they say.

But the tithe was hardly a gift. The tithe was much more like a tax. Offerings were above the tithe. Almost certainly, the gifts given by the people in the Temple courts that day when Jesus saw the widow were separate from the tithe. If the widow gave all she had, it was far more than a tithe of what she brought in by her work. Zacchaeus didn't mention his tithe. As a Jew, he was expected to give the percentage. What he offered to Jesus was far more than a tenth.

There is some debate within the community of grace teachers about the tithe. Some think that the tithe should continue as a way for people to connect with the giving love of God. As we give, He gives more, they say. Other teachers are adamant that the tithe is part of the Old Covenant Law, not something binding on believers today. Some suggest that both are true, that the tithe is not binding but is a good guideline for believers.

Believers are left with a burden. They know they are called to give, but don't know how or how much. Do we just skim a percentage off the top and consider ourselves covered? Or is there something more? And, what if ten percent seems like too much or too little? How much should go to the church, and what about other causes? We want to give, even give generously, but we are puzzled. What does God expect of us?

Many believers associate giving with guilt, fear, and manipulation. The church has built ministries and buildings on the giving of its people. Churches, missionary organizations, and para-church ministries depend on the giving of the people. That giving must be maintained, even increased. But so many preachers and fund-raisers have used coercive tactics that the topic of giving is unwelcome, whether from the pulpit, the mail, or the Scriptures.

One of the psychological principles the church has ignored is that guilt is a very costly motivator. Those who are motivated by guilt or fear feel abused. They may respond according to the desire of the one with the guilt message, but they will seek ways to separate from that message. They will not "buy into" the message or mission but will do the minimum to get away from the manipulation. Today, the coercive tactics of fundraising are encountered daily by those in and out of the church. Givers build up resistance against such messages and, perhaps appropriately, ministries and causes suffer. Once givers find the strength to defy the manipulation, they build their immunity to pleas for help. Guilt produces resistance.

Yet, we are called to care for the hurting, further the ministry of the gospel, and make a difference through our giving. How do we do this while avoiding the guilt and anger produced by the constant manipulation of the fund-raisers?

The answer is in something I call, *Giving Grace*. What have we learned through the previous chapters of this book? That whatever God asks of us, He is ready to provide for us. That we can look to Him for active guidance and provision. That God is real and alive and loves us. Even our giving is part of His grace.

Let's settle the tithing question. The tithe was part of the Old Testament Law. Before the law was given, Abraham gave a tenth of what he had gained in battle to Melchizedek, the priest of God. He did that because his heart was moved in gratitude for what God had done. Later, a system of tithes was set up under the law to pay for both religious and governmental needs. The tithe of Abraham was an offering from the heart. The tithe under the law was a type of tax.

We are no longer under the law. Paul makes that clear over and over. There is no burden of ten percent laid on believers. If you respond to the goodness of God by giving a gift to a ministry He has called you or others to do, your gift, like Abraham's tenth, is an offering. If you want to determine the amount of that gift by a percentage, you are welcome to do so. But there is nothing in the New Testament that requires a tithe from you or from anyone under grace.

In fact, Paul makes that clear as well. He says,

> *So let each one give as he purposes in his heart, not grudgingly or of necessity; for God loves a cheerful giver.*
> *2 Corinthians 9:7*

Not "of necessity." In other words, not because someone placed the burden on you. Manipulation or guilt causes us to give "grudgingly," without joy or heart. As Paul wrote to his friends in Corinth, he didn't want them to feel pressure from him. He asked them to look to the Lord and give as their hearts were led. Here's the context:

> *But this I say: He who sows sparingly will also reap sparingly, and he who sows bountifully will also reap bountifully. So let each one give as he purposes in his heart, not grudgingly or of necessity; for God loves a cheerful giver. And God is able to make all grace abound toward you, that you, always having all sufficiency in all things, may have an abundance for every good work.*
> *2 Corinthians 9:6-8*

Paul knew the promise of God, that God rewards faithfulness, which simply means to trust in Him, and that He provides all that He asks of us. God will give to us sufficiently so that we can give, and there will be enough "for every good work."

I have a good pastor friend who led a large congregation through several building programs. Each time they were able to build without long term debt. I heard him come to the congregation and say, "Just ask the Lord what He would have you give, do what He says, and there will always be enough." A gentle message leading people to the Lord.

The tithe is mentioned only twice in the New Testament, in Luke 11:42 and Matthew 23:23, as Jesus scolds the Pharisees for maintaining the precise rules of the law while ignoring the call of God to their hearts. It isn't mentioned as a negative, but as something that is insufficient. The Pharisees thought they were being more spiritual by tithing in more specific areas, but they were just showing their lack of connection to the heart of God. Otherwise, Paul does not speak of tithing. Nor does John, or Peter, or even James. It simply is not a New Covenant teaching.

So, if we are not required or expected to give as those under the law, how do we give as people under grace? There is a very clear answer: ask.

I am often amazed at how we complicate the things of the Lord. Even the Scriptures are sometimes complicated to the point of being indecipherable. We read part of 2 Corinthians 9 above, but there are a couple more verses that are important for us.

Now may He who supplies seed to the sower, and bread for food, supply and multiply the seed you

*have sown and increase the fruits of your right-
eousness,
while you are enriched in everything for all liberality, which causes thanksgiving through us to God.
For the administration of this service not only
supplies the needs of the saints, but also is abounding through many thanksgivings to God, while,
through the proof of this ministry, they glorify
God for the obedience of your confession to the
gospel of Christ, and for your liberal sharing with
them and all men, and by their prayer for you, who
long for you because of the exceeding grace of God
in you. Thanks be to God for His indescribable gift!
2 Corinthians 9:10-15*

Some modern translations are more helpful, but
let's sort this out. It is God who gives to us all that we
need. He provides seed for the farmer and bread for
those who have mouths to feed. He is our Provider.
Paul prays that God would generously provide for the
people in Corinth so they would have plenty to pass
on to others. He asks that they would be "enriched in
everything for all liberality." In other words, that God
would give them enough to be generous with others.
From the blessings God gives to them, they distribute
blessings to others. That's all Paul expects from them.

Now, notice that he is not manipulating them,
not moving them with guilt or duty, but showing
them that God will use them as channels for His ben-
evolence. The rest of the passage is about the community joy that is built as one group is used to bless
another. Paul received their gifts and distributed
them again. And, he says, the process of sharing shows

"the exceeding grace of God in you."

Grace, the activity of God, is revealed as we take the blessings God gives to us and share them with others. This is not sacrificial giving. This is not a tithe. This is giving from the heart as we respond to the Lord. That's giving grace.

How do you know how much or when to give? You ask. In all the aspects of grace we have considered to this point, we are called to ask for what we need. If you believe the Lord is leading you to give, ask when and how much. If you wonder whether the Lord is leading you to give, ask Him. Trust that He will answer you. Listen. He is the Lord and you are the servant. If the Master supplies all your needs, then let Him provide what you need to give and let Him tell you when and how.

Once you understand that giving is an opportunity for you to participate in His work, you begin to see the joy in it. Our God is active in the lives of His people. He testifies to His love by providing in times of need. He connects us so that we can share a testimony to His kindness. The receiver is blessed by the gift. The giver is blessed to be the witness and the servant. Both are able to point to what God has done.

What does this look like in practice? Imagine, with no burden, asking the Lord if and how you should contribute. We are bombarded these days with requests. We can't harden our hearts to all of them. Nor can we research every one to see who deserves an offering. Instead, we can look to the Master to lead us. Sometimes, that will mean we walk or scroll past the request. Sometimes, that will mean we contribute.

Most of us who are on social media have to scroll past numerous requests each day. I am sure that many are good causes. The need is real, and the money will be handled responsibly. Still, I scroll past. But I have a "friend" (person I have connected with on social media, but never met in person) who has a call from the Lord to help a group of orphans in Indonesia. Now, frankly, I don't like what this man teaches. I think he is wrong about many things. I might even write a note to counter his teaching. But, a month or so ago, he wrote about a need the orphans had, and the Lord prompted me to send a gift. Not much, but a contribution toward a project that would lift the lives of these children in the name of Jesus. The gift I sent would not have been enough to accomplish the project, but the accumulated gifts of people moved by the Lord were enough. Besides that, a good number of people have been moved to pray for these children. The man who was used to carry the gifts and do the project was blessed by the response. The givers were all blessed to be a part of something so far from home, something personal and practical. And, of course, the orphans and those who cared for them were blessed by a positive change in their lives. And Jesus was glorified. That was a win all the way around. No guilt. No manipulation. The person who carried the gift barely factored in. Just Jesus using His people to bless others.

There is a miracle in giving because the hand of God is in it. Five loaves and two fish fed 5000 or more people. No one yet has explained how that happened. One small contribution made a great difference. As we listen to the Lord and give as He leads, the increase is accomplished by Him. God does His work. A gift of twenty dollars from you builds classrooms for orphans across the ocean. A gift of a hundred dollars builds a church in your town. A gift of five dollars feeds the hungry man on the street. God does His work!

I have heard people say that the tithe is a "Biblical principle." When I say that tithing is not binding on those under grace, they try to use all the promises of the Old Testament in support of the tithe. But those promises are in support of the true Biblical principle, that those who give are blessed.

> *The generous soul will be made rich, and he who waters will also be watered himself.*
> *Proverbs 11:25*

To support the tithe, teachers tell us that no one can out-give God. That's true, whether you tithe or not. All good things come from His hand. We would have nothing apart from His kindness. So, whatever we give and whatever we use for ourselves have come from Him. No one can out-give God.

Jesus taught the principle of giving when He said, "Give, and it will be given to you." In the Sermon on the Mount He warned His people against giving for recognition. The blessing comes when you give as a channel from the Lord.

> *But when you do a charitable deed, do not let your*
> *left hand know what your right hand is doing, that*
> *your charitable deed may be in secret; and your*
> *Father who sees in secret will Himself reward you*
> *openly.*
> *Matthew 6:3-4*

Giving from the heart carries its own reward. We are blessed as we give, but Paul warned us about giving without love.

> *And though I bestow all my goods to feed the poor,*
> *and though I give my body to be burned, but have*
> *not love, it profits me nothing.*
> *1 Corinthians 13:3*

Giving far beyond the tithe to the point of the greatest personal sacrifice brings no reward if love is not the motivation. Love for Jesus. Love for those Jesus loves. Our hearts are to be connected to our giving.

Grace is a matter of the heart. Believers live in relationship with the Lord who loves them. The more we learn about and experience that love, the more love we have for Him and for others. We are connected to Jesus at the heart.

As you experience giving grace, there will be no guilt or sacrifice or pain. You do not need to fear giving. Instead, as you participate with what Jesus does for His people, allowing Him to work through you whenever He wishes, knowing that anything He asks of you will be provided for you, the joy of giving will be yours.

David, the king of Israel, was moved by God to build a temple in Jerusalem. But, when the time came, the task was given to his son, Solomon. David set aside a great amount of his personal wealth for the building, and the people gave generously. The Temple would be a testimony to the provision and greatness of God. And David was humbled to see what God was going to do and how He did it.

> *But who am I, and who are my people, that we should be able to offer so willingly as this? For all things come from You, and of Your own we have given You.*
> *1 Chronicles 29:14*

The offerings were far more than anyone could have expected, because God gave more than anyone expected. And those who gave were blessed.

That's giving grace.

LOVING GRACE

It is reported that Confucius, the Chinese philosopher who lived about 500 years before Christ, said, "What you do not want done to yourself, do not do to others."

Socrates, the great philosopher who lived in Greece nearly 400 years before Jesus, once said, "What stirs your anger when done to you by others, that do not do to others."

The great Jewish rabbi, Hillel, who lived about the same time as the Lord said it this way, "Do not do to thy neighbor what is hateful to thyself."

Now some people might hear these words and be impressed that the Golden Rule was not original with Jesus. Maybe He was just copying what these great men had said. Their words sound just like His, don't they?

But they are not like His. The words of Jesus are different. You see, all the rest are in the negative. We are not to hurt others. We are not to be cruel to others. These admonitions are negative.

What Jesus said was far more difficult, far more convicting. He said, "Do unto others as you would have them do unto you." This is in the positive sense.

It is far easier to avoid others altogether than it is to love them. The words of the other great thinkers might move us away from aggressive behavior toward others, but they do not call us to love. They might move us toward a sense of fairness and justice, but there is no kindness, no mercy, in those words.

Jesus wanted us to love others. He commanded us to love others throughout the Scriptures. Look sometime at the great chapter on love, 1 Corinthians 13, and you will see the depth of the love we are supposed to have for others. This love is only possible through the grace of our Lord.

No matter how much we learn about love, loving is still hard. There are those who seem unlovable. There are those we really don't want to know, let alone love. Then there are others we know too well to love. Yet, all of these we are called to love.

Of all the commands given to the people of God, the command to love may be both the most important and the most difficult. To love is to go outside ourselves, to look at and care for others and their needs. The flesh cannot love others. Love is the purest expression of the life of Jesus Christ within us.

Of course, as I say that, we all know that unbelievers can love, right? Let's be honest. Unbelievers love their children. Some even love their parents and their neighbors. In fact, some unbelievers are more loving than some of God's people. I know that some would suggest that their love isn't true love, but we have to admit that some of our love isn't true love either. In fact, what we call love in our lives is not much different from what they call love.

So, if even pagans can love, how can we say that love is something only found in Jesus? The answer is in the love we don't like to talk about. True love is when we love the unlovable.

> "But I say to you who hear: Love your enemies, do good to those who hate you, bless those who curse you, and pray for those who spitefully use you. To him who strikes you on the one cheek, offer the other also. And from him who takes away your cloak, do not withhold your tunic either. Give to everyone who asks of you. And from him who takes away your goods do not ask them back. And just as you want men to do to you, you also do to them likewise.
> "But if you love those who love you, what credit is that to you? For even sinners love those who love them. And if you do good to those who do good to you, what credit is that to you? For even sinners do the same. And if you lend to those from whom you hope to receive back, what credit is that to you? For even sinners lend to sinners to receive as much back. But love your enemies, do good, and lend, hoping for nothing in return; and your reward will be great, and you will be sons of the Most High. For He is kind to the unthankful and evil. Therefore be merciful, just as your Father also is merciful."
> Luke 6:27-36

Yes, the pagans love each other. They do love those who love them in return. They are kind to those who will advance their agenda. They give generously to meet the needs of their own hearts. But we are asked to love the unlovable. We are told to love those who will not love us back, who might even do wrong to us in return for our kindness. We are to follow the example of Jesus.

He loves everyone. He loved us while we were His enemies. He loved us when we ignored Him; and when we disobeyed Him; and when we took advantage of His kindness; and when we laughed at those who loved Him; and when we said we wanted nothing to do with Him. He still loved us. Are we really supposed to love like that?

> This is My commandment, that you love one an-
> other as I have loved you.
> John 15:12

Yes, we really are supposed to love like that. Is it impossible? Yes—for our flesh.

Jesus gave us a wonderful example of love in the story of the Good Samaritan. You remember the story. It was prompted by a question from a young lawyer, a student of the law. He knew there was something lacking in his heart. When he claimed to have kept all the commandments throughout his life, Jesus knew the truth. He wasn't really bragging. He genuinely tried to be good. But there was something missing. Love.

Jesus told the story of a certain man who "fell among thieves." In other words, he was mugged. As he lay hurting, people walked by him. They ignored his needs, even though he was one of their own people.

He might have paid them. He might have rewarded their kindness. But they walked by because they were afraid of the cost to themselves.

Finally, a Samaritan man noticed the need and came to help. Now, we must understand that the Jews hated the Samaritans. It was very likely that this hurting man would turn against the Samaritan as soon as he was well. He might have rejected the kindness. He might have pushed the Good Samaritan away.

None of that mattered. The man was hurting and needed help. Love demanded kindness and caring. The Samaritan was good because he followed the command to love his neighbor.

We are commanded to love. It doesn't matter whether the person is lovable, we must love. How do we do such a thing? Only by the grace of the Lord; perhaps only through *Loving Grace*.

I don't know why but it seems like the holidays often test our love. Perhaps it is because we get together with people we can normally avoid. Perhaps it is because the season is already filled with stress. Perhaps it is because we are often self-centered at holiday times. Whatever it is, love seems to be tested at the holidays.

You know what I mean. You hate to get together with a certain person because you know what he or she will say (or maybe because you don't know what that person will say). You get unending phone calls asking for money. The mail is full of all kinds of tricks to get you to give. You feel like you have to match gifts with people. You give gifts that cost you money and time, and you just know they won't really be appreciated. Sometimes the holidays get filled with everything but love.

Let's be honest. There are people who are hard to love. Some people try very hard, it seems, to be insensitive or unkind. There are people who don't particularly like you or me. Listen carefully: these are the people Jesus wants us to love.

What's the big deal with us loving each other? We like each other already. We are friends. What's the big deal with being loving toward your family? That's supposed to be easy because they love you in return. The hard ones are those who don't love you back. The hard ones are those into whom you can pour all kinds of love and get nothing in return. That's when love is something special, according to Jesus.

And that's when love is impossible. There is nothing in you that wants to love someone like that, at least nothing in your flesh. Your feelings are natural. When you want to stay away, when you want to avoid that person, when you just wish you didn't have to deal with the problem, those are normal human emotions. The flesh doesn't love anyone who doesn't pay back.

So, if those feelings are normal and we are still commanded to love that person, what's the secret? Well, we are to reach out to the one Person who is not normal. Jesus is without sin. No stain of the flesh is on Him. He loves perfectly. He can love that person through you.

You see, love is an active verb. It is something we

do. Love is not a feeling we have toward someone. That's the world's kind of love, isn't it? I love you because you make me feel good. I feel good when I am with you, so I must love you. That's the world's kind of love.

The love of the Lord Jesus Christ for us is the love that reaches out to enemies, to the unlovable. Only His love in us and through us can move us to <u>do</u> love toward others, especially those who are hard to love.

Is His grace enough even for this? Can Jesus Christ love that person in your life? Of course, He already loves that person, doesn't He? His love reaches out to everyone. When the Scripture says, "God so loved the world," it is referring to that person in your life. No one is excluded from the love of the Lord. Not even that person.

Pray for loving grace. We could call it "the grace to love." Pray that the Lord would use your life to express His love for that person. Then act according to that love.

There are two things to remember. First, you don't have to come up with the love from yourself. Don't worry, you can't. It isn't there. He will give that love when you ask for it. You probably won't feel more loving toward the person. In fact, you might not see a great deal of change. But, in response to your prayer, you will be sharing the love of the Lord when you visit with that person or reach out to him or her.

Another thing: if that love, that kindness, is rejected, just remember that it wasn't from you. It wasn't your love that was rejected, it was the love of Jesus. What a sad thing to reject His love! Yet, we understand that because most of us did that in our lives. We pushed Him away for a time. Your person might do the same thing, no matter how much Jesus uses you to reach out.

If you take the rejection personally, it may have been your love that reached out to the person. Instead, remember that Jesus has a lot more love where that came from, and He is very generous with His love. You can go back again and again. If that person wants to reject your kindness, remember that they are rejecting His kindness.

You see, grace is the wonderful, powerful, generous Lord reaching down to us in our need. When we find it hard to love, He has plenty of love to give. All you do to receive love, enough love to get through anything, is to bow before Him in submission and humility and ask. Then receive what He gives.

Does that sound too hard—too easy? It is the truth. All we need is found in our Lord. His grace is sufficient for all our needs.

SUFFERING GRACE

Thomas Wolfe gets the credit for a familiar saying. He considered it to be a summary of the fatalistic philosophy of the Bible book of Ecclesiastes. He wrote, in "You Can't Go Home Again":

> *Man was born to live, to suffer, and to die, and what befalls him is a tragic lot. There is no denying this in the final end. But we must, dear Fox, deny it all along the way.*[3]

In other words, we can't allow ourselves to become fatalists. Even if we feel that every gravestone should bear the words, "We are born, we suffer, and we die." As we go through our days, we must live as though there is hope and promise, some good to find and hold.

You know, the Bible is honest. I have always been impressed with the simple honesty expressed by the words of Scripture. Preachers and teachers may twist the teachings of the Bible to sound uncaring or wrong, but the text is bluntly honest. Perhaps one of the most honest people Jesus encountered was the father of the young man who suffered from seizures. In Mark

9 we read the story:

> And when He came to the disciples, He saw a
> great multitude around them, and scribes disput-
> ing with them. Immediately, when they saw Him,
> all the people were greatly amazed, and running to
> Him, greeted Him. And He asked the scribes, "What
> are you discussing with them?" Then one of the
> crowd answered and said, "Teacher, I brought You
> my son, who has a mute spirit. And wherever it
> seizes him, it throws him down; he foams at the
> mouth, gnashes his teeth, and becomes rigid. So I
> spoke to Your disciples, that they should cast it out,
> but they could not." He answered him and said, "O
> faithless generation, how long shall I be with you?
> How long shall I bear with you? Bring him to Me."
> Then they brought him to Him. And when he saw
> Him, immediately the spirit convulsed him, and he
> fell on the ground and wallowed, foaming at the
> mouth. So He asked his father, "How long has this
> been happening to him?" And he said, "From child-
> hood. And often he has thrown him both into the
> fire and into the water to destroy him. But if You
> can do anything, have compassion on us and help
> us." Jesus said to him, "If you can believe, all things
> are possible to him who believes." Immediately the
> father of the child cried out and said with tears,
> "Lord, I believe; help my unbelief!" When Jesus saw
> that the people came running together, He rebuked
> the unclean spirit, saying to it, "Deaf and dumb
> spirit, I command you, come out of him and enter
> him no more!" Then the spirit cried out, convulsed
> him greatly, and came out of him. And he became
> as one dead, so that many said, "He is dead." But
> Jesus took him by the hand and lifted him up, and

> *he arose. And when He had come into the house,*
> *His disciples asked Him privately, "Why could we*
> *not cast it out?" So He said to them, "This kind can*
> *come out by nothing but prayer and fasting."*
> *Mark 9:14-29*

This is a story of suffering, not just the suffering of the boy, but of the father who was forced to watch helplessly as his son struggled. Today, we would call him a "caregiver." His statement of faith is so powerful. He brings his son to Jesus. He looks to Jesus for a miracle. Since he was a child, the boy suffered these seizures, probably something like epilepsy. It was clear to the father, and to Jesus, that the boy struggled against an evil spirit.

Now, I know there are many questions about the cause of the boy's struggle. But I want to look simply at the father's suffering. He brings his son to Jesus in hope, probably trying yet another cure, seeking yet another miracle. The disciples had tried to help, but they couldn't. I don't doubt that the father had gone through whatever was suggested by the scribes and Pharisees. He was willing to try anything, so he went to Jesus.

When Jesus told him to believe, the father sobbed. He said, "Lord, I believe; help my unbelief!"

Now, that we understand. In 1977, Philip Yancy wrote a book called, "Where Is God When It Hurts?" Forty-two years ago, and the book is still in print, still popular. It's a good book, but I think its popularity comes from the title. Who hasn't asked that question? When we hurt, we wonder where God is. We want to know He is there.

The father brought his son to Jesus. He looked to Jesus for help. Simply and powerfully, Jesus cast the demon from the boy and gave the miracle the father needed. The suffering ended.

I suggest that this story is as important for what it doesn't say as for anything else. Notice that Jesus speaks bluntly. The father responds in the same way. The truth is that both the father and the son were suffering. The truth was that the answer was to be found in Jesus.

But why didn't Jesus remind the man that suffering was good? That's what we have been taught. That's what preachers always say. Suffering draws us to our knees. Suffering is good for us. Jesus suffered and so should we, they say. Those who do right will suffer, they say.

We used to know people who wanted to suffer. They looked for opportunities to suffer for Jesus. They thought suffering was a way of gaining more spiritual points. They wanted God to see them faithful during their suffering. Their suffering would become something they could boast about.

Now, I have looked through the words of Jesus carefully. I might have missed something, but I couldn't find any place where Jesus tells a person to just keep going in their suffering and consider it a gift from the Lord. No, in every case, Jesus healed and delivered. The only suffering Jesus talked about was His own. He would suffer, and He would suffer for us.

At the same time, the Scripture does not say that

Jesus healed everyone. There were many at the pool in John 5, but only one was healed. That man had suffered for thirty-eight years. His healing became a source of frustration and scandal for the Pharisees and scribes. They knew he had been healed, but it was on the Sabbath. Jesus challenged the traditional teachings with power and authority.

The Bible is an honest book, an honest word from the Lord who loves us. God knows about suffering. He knows that suffering is real, and He knows that it hurts.

So, how do we handle suffering under grace? We look to the Lord for *Suffering Grace*. If grace is practical, it should somehow relate to our suffering. Those who teach the law would have us work harder, be more obedient, grow in our faith, if we want to avoid or be released from suffering. They may not have the right answers, but they have answers. They tell us that suffering brings us closer to the goals God has for our lives. They tell us that suffering is a blessing. They tell us to endure until our efforts warrant healing. These answers are far from comforting.

Let's ask three questions. First, what is suffering? Then, where does suffering come from? Finally, what are we supposed to do about suffering? With the grace and love of Jesus as our foundation, we should find some honest and helpful answers.

Suffering, in the New Testament, is almost always a type of "negative passion." The Greek words stem from some form of *pathos*, which suggests strong sensation or feeling. When translated as "suffering" they can refer to things like heartache, pain, or anxiety. There is another use of the word, "suffer," which means to endure or allow, perhaps tolerate. We can see the connection, but our concern involves the struggle of intense physical or emotional pain. Both the father and the son in the story were suffering.

Suffering has been a part of the human condition since the Fall. In our day, we do as much as possible to avoid suffering. So much so that we hear complaints of suffering from those who seem to know almost nothing about it. I would suggest that there are three levels of suffering in our lives: dissatisfaction, discomfort, and distress.

For some, the dissatisfaction of not getting what they want is a level of suffering hard to endure. If they can't eat at the same time every day or can't find a parking space or don't like their latest haircut, they think they are suffering. If you listen to them complain, you realize they don't know what suffering really is. The truth is that we don't get everything we want in life. In fact, a certain dissatisfaction with our situation is normal. We don't like our politicians or the decisions they make. We don't like the prices at the store. We don't like busy roads or long sermons. None of this is suffering.

The next level may not be as distinct. One person's discomfort may be another person's pain. We know that some people can handle a great deal of pain and still function. Others seem to be able to handle much less, or their pain is greater even with the same cause. I have always been impressed that some can work through a migraine, when I am debilitated by mine. We take medications and have surgeries to minimize our physical discomfort. We adapt to a noisy work environment or life in a narcissistic relationship. At least we try. While some would consider discomfort to be suffering, and we might do well not to argue, it does not seem that this is what most people would mean by the word.

When pain becomes an intense daily struggle, when the discomfort is chronic and serious, we look for answers. The obvious question is what to do, but under that is why the struggle has come. Some teach that suffering comes from sin. I have heard teachers trace all suffering, particularly serious and chronic pain, back to sin in the person's life. Others say that God sends suffering to teach us, to help us grow. And, again, they suggest that we should be grateful for any suffering we have to endure.

So, let's limit our definition of suffering to this intense and lasting pain or grief or disability. The son suffered this way as he dealt with his seizures. The father suffered this way as he searched for ways to help his boy. Some suffer this way today because of diseases or accidents or genetic disorders. Some people struggle for years. We don't know how old the boy was, only that he was the son of the man who brought him. When Jesus asked how long the boy had the demon, the father answered that he had it since childhood or infancy. He could be a teenager, or he might be in his thirties. In any case, he and his father had struggled a long time. The man who sat by the pool in John 5 had waited thirty-eight years for deliverance. When we talk about suffering, we have to include the duration.

The reason the duration is important is that most of the solutions offered have been proved insufficient. The cancer, the paralysis, the chronic pain—they are not going away on their own, and nothing has seemed to work. When the "what-to-do" has been asked without an answer, the "why" is a normal question.

So, let's ask it. Does God send suffering? For the law-teacher, cause and effect is primary. If you have an effect, whether it is positive or negative, there must be a cause. Pain comes out of sin. Pleasure comes from obedience. Simple. But Job was a faithful man who went beyond others in his devotion. His loss was almost unbearable, and his suffering was intense. What did Job do wrong that caused his suffering? Nothing. The text makes this clear. Job suffered because Satan attacked him.

Does God send suffering? Under grace, the answer must be, "No." It is true that certain behaviors may lead to suffering. Drinking and driving. Extended drug use or promiscuity or overeating. These things can cause great pain and much suffering. But the cause and effect process must be understood. God does not send a car accident because someone has been drinking. Nor does He send sexual disease because someone has broken marriage vows. The most obvious evidence of this is the pain that can be suffered by those innocent of the sin but caught in the situation.

The people in the other car. The wife of the adulterer. The widows and the orphans. If God sends suffering because of sin, why does He send it to them? The natural result of sin is suffering. God warns us against these things because He loves us and doesn't want us to suffer.

No, God is not the source of our suffering. There may be rare times found in the pages of Scripture where God sent trouble to turn the hearts of certain people. But that is not the normal cause of suffering. Suffering is part of this broken world. Disease exists because of sin, but not because of the specific sins you and I have done. Disease is part of the general effect sin has had on the world. Things are not the same as God made them in the beginning. Creation was broken when the heart of humankind was broken. Diseases, accidents, wars, abuse, famines, natural disasters—these all come from the brokenness of the world, not from the hand of God.

Suffering is a natural result of the effect of sin on the world. The cruelties of nature are obvious to anyone who watches. The little bird suffers as the larger bird feeds on it. The larger bird suffers when it cannot find enough to eat. When it dies, other creatures eat. Death, pain, and suffering are natural, but they were not part of the plan. Sin broke the plan and broke the world.

The next question, for those who admit that God does not send suffering, is why God allows suffering. We believe that God can intervene. Jesus healed the son who suffered from seizures. Jesus healed the man who had waited beside the pool. If suffering is a natural part of a broken world, why doesn't God intervene on behalf of those who trust in Him? He could stop it from touching us, or He could end it quickly when it does touch us. Why doesn't He?

Well, again, let's be honest. Most of us have seen the protecting hand of God intervene for us. A car accident that didn't happen or one in which we didn't get hurt. A disease that passes by our home. A new job that comes as the old one is lost. We have seen His deliverance. Because the suffering didn't happen, we tend to discount these things. It is the grace of a loving Father that allows us to avoid so many difficulties without being aware or even properly grateful.

And we have seen His deliverance. A surgery that ended the disability. Medicine that took away the pain. Perhaps even a miracle that brought our healing. We have sinned in ways that could have led to serious suffering, but He has protected us. We have walked in safety through dangers, often without even seeing them. The hand of God is strong and active on our behalf.

Suffering for most of us, even in this broken world, is not normal. We cry out in the pain and struggle partly because it is unusual or unexpected. Our God is protecting us and delivering us, perhaps far more often than we realize. At the same time, suffering is with us in this world, even for believers. We can't ignore the struggle of some just because we may not be suffering now.

In those times when suffering comes to us, we

would like to know why. If God didn't send it, then why does He allow it? Why didn't He protect us? The answers we are most often given sound just like reasons people give to say God sends suffering. There are three common answers.

Suffering comes from sin, they say. God allows suffering to get us back on track, to draw attention to our sin. If He doesn't send it, He at least doesn't deliver us from it until we learn our lesson. Suffering is like a painful barrier for those who stray from the path. Stay in the middle of the right way and every-thing will be fine. Step off to the side and feel the pain.

Or they say suffering comes to draw us closer to God. He allows us to hurt so we will come to Him in our need. Unbelievers can find God in their suffering. Believers find the presence of God to be even more real in those times. Suffering allows us to know God better, to identify with Christ in His pains, and to seek Him in more areas of our lives. Aside from the concern that this doesn't fit well with our ideas of love, it is troubling for many to think that God would use such pain to manipulate us.

Another reason often given is that our faith be-comes an example for others as we suffer. It is a tes-timony to the love of God for us to remain faithful when we hurt. To have a positive demeanor and kind words during pain suggests a strength that comes from somewhere outside ourselves. Others will see that and give glory to the Lord.

Now, there is certainly some truth in each of these. There are Scriptures to support all of them.

Wrong behavior, as mentioned earlier, often leads to suffering. God may allow that suffering so that we learn. Going through a time of suffering causes us to take our eyes off the busyness of this world and look to the Lord. Even as we look to Him for help, we draw nearer. And most of us have known someone whose faith and gentle kindness during suffering is a testimony of God's power. Yet, most of those who suffer find these answers less than comforting.

Job's friends tried hard to convince him that his suffering came from sin, but we know from the story that it did not. Telling someone that sin is the cause of their pain may move them to repentance, but what if the pain doesn't go away? If they acknowledge that they were off the track, wandering into evil, and then make serious and lasting changes, will the problems stop? If they don't stop, is it because God allows the suffering to continue as punishment? Or to drive the point home? Or is there something more? And, didn't Jesus take the punishment for our sin on Himself? No believer faces punishment for sin under grace. We may face earthly consequences for wrong behavior, but not punishment for sin from God.

When we give sufferers platitudes and pat answers, we do more to confuse and discourage than to help. Job's friends shared the answers they had learned, but those answers were neither right nor comforting. The only thing that comforted Job was his conversation with the Lord. Yes, it was intimidating. Job found himself humbled when he asked his questions, but God spoke truth to Job's heart and brought both healing and restoration.

Under grace, to be honest, we have fewer answers. Under grace, the platitudes are set aside. The proof texts and traditional wisdom are put away. We don't say those answers are not true, but we have a better answer.

You see, the grace of God is found in Jesus. Sometimes we say that grace is a Person. God's love came to us in Jesus. Jesus is real, and He is with us, and He cares for us. The best thing we can do for someone who is suffering is to bring them to Jesus. The best thing we can do for ourselves when we are suffering is to find and spend time with Jesus.

Pat answers and proof texts are nice, but there is nothing like a real Person in our suffering. We know that family and friends can provide true comfort during our pain, but their ability to help is so limited. Jesus is the answer we need. Jesus is the friend, the brother, the Lord who sits with us.

What do we do about suffering under grace? How does grace deal with our pain? The answer is Jesus. Not the idea of Jesus. Not the teachings of Jesus. Jesus as a real and present Person.

The father took his son to Jesus. The disciples knew about miracles, and they prayed, but they couldn't help. The scribes and Pharisees knew doctrine and Scripture, but they couldn't help. The father didn't know what Jesus would do, but he took his son to Jesus anyway.

When you come to Jesus in your suffering, you may not know what He will do. He may heal you with a miraculous touch. He may send you back to the doctors. He may sit with you through the pain. But He will be with you. He may tell you that your suffering is the result of your sin. He might. Or He might say that it is for the glory of God. Or He may tell you that you will learn something through the trouble that will be useful later. He may tell you these things. If He tells you, you will find comfort. He may tell you nothing, but still sit with you through it all.

Over the years I have asked believers a question. It may not be a comforting question, but it helps to bring things back into focus. Rather than offer the traditional answers, I will ask this: What if Jesus appeared to you and asked your permission to let you go through this trouble? What if He assured you that it had a real purpose for His work or for your life? If He came, looked you in the eyes, reminded you that He loved you and would be with you through the whole process, would you give your permission? I have never had a believer say no. All, when thinking about Jesus, would give their permission. So, the only difference between what you have right now and what I just described is that He didn't ask. He is your Lord, but He is also your friend. You never walk alone, no matter how much it hurts.

Under grace, we remember that Jesus is a real Person who loves us. It isn't about rules and sayings and traditional answers. It is about Him, just Him and us. In that hospital bed, Jesus is there. In the dark of night when the tears flow, Jesus is there. In the pain, in the worry, in the fear, in the suffering—Jesus is there.

Grace is about Jesus.

****

[3] Wolfe, Thomas. You Can't Go Home Again. New York: Harper and Row Publications, 1935. p. 737

SERVING GRACE

Every young student should know of Isaac Newton's famed encounter with a falling apple, whether it really happened or not. Newton discovered and introduced the laws of gravity in the 1600s, which revolutionized astronomical studies. But few know that if it weren't for Edmund Halley, the world might never have learned from Newton.

It was Halley who challenged Newton to think through his original notions. Halley corrected Newton's mathematical errors and prepared geometrical figures to support his discoveries. Halley coaxed the hesitant Newton to write his great work, *Mathematical Principals of Natural Philosophy*. Halley edited and supervised the publication and financed its printing, even though Newton was wealthier and easily could have afforded the printing costs. Historians call it one of the most selfless examples in the annals of science.

Newton began almost immediately to reap the rewards of prominence; Halley received little credit. He did use the principles to predict the orbit and return of the comet that would later bear his name, but only after his death did he receive any acclaim and, because the comet only returns every seventy-six years, the recognition is rather infrequent. Halley remained a devoted scientist who didn't care who received the credit if the cause was being advanced.

There is a great blessing for those who are willing to serve. To serve the Lord and to serve others is, perhaps, the greatest call on the Christian life. We have considered the call to love. Now we focus on the activity of love, which is service. If we love God, we will serve Him. If we love others, we will serve them.

Certainly, this is the model our Lord has given to us. In the message of the gospel, we cannot help but see the great act of service our Lord did for us. Motivated by His amazing love, He humbled Himself and became like us so that He, by His own sacrificial service, could give us eternal life.

Not only that, as wonderful as it was, He also showed us service through His earthly life. He washed His disciples' feet. He served them at Passover. He fed the multitude and healed their diseases. His whole earthly life was a life of service.

So, we also are called to serve. There is a clear command to us that we should serve the Lord.

> And now, Israel, what does the LORD your God require of you, but to fear the LORD your God, to walk in all His ways and to love Him, to serve the LORD your God with all your heart and with all your soul.
> Deuteronomy 10:12

To serve Him with all your heart and soul. That's

the command. And it isn't a hard command for us, is it? After all, we know that our eternal future is a gift from His love. To serve the Lord is a joy to us.

Oh, I know that there are still some distractions and temptations in our hearts. But almost every Christian would like to serve the Lord faithfully. How can we respond to His great love for us in any other way? If we belong to Him, we want to serve Him and offer many good works to His glory. It isn't just that we want to hear the words, "Well done!" when we arrive in Heaven. It isn't just that we look forward to the rewards for faithful service. It is that we love Him and want to show our love for Him by our gifts.

Serving the Lord and serving others is an important part of the Christian life. In fact, if we put it in terms of love (and service is simply love in action), then serving the Lord and serving others is the central call of the Christian life.

The command to serve the Lord and the Lord only is so strong that great blessings and curses are tied to it. In Deuteronomy, Moses gives the word of the Lord to the people:

> 'And it shall be that if you earnestly obey My commandments which I command you today, to love the LORD your God and serve Him with all your heart and with all your soul, then I will give you the rain for your land in its season, the early rain and the latter rain, that you may gather in your grain, your new wine, and your oil. And I will send grass in your fields for your livestock, that you may eat and be filled.' Take heed to yourselves,

> *lest your heart be deceived, and you turn aside and serve other gods and worship them, lest the LORD'S anger be aroused against you, and He shut up the heavens so that there be no rain, and the land yield no produce, and you perish quickly from the good land which the LORD is giving you. Deuteronomy 11:13-17*

In other words, the Lord will make it worth your while to serve Him faithfully and sincerely. If you do not serve Him, however, you will serve evil, and service to evil will have negative consequences.

You cannot do both, according to the Lord.

> *No one can serve two masters; for either he will hate the one and love the other, or else he will be loyal to the one and despise the other. You cannot serve God and mammon.*
> *Matthew 6:24*

So, we must serve the Lord. It is commanded, and it is expected. It is also the joy and privilege of our lives. However, before you run out to serve the Lord there is something you need to know. In order to please the Lord with your service, you need what I will call *Serving Grace.*

You see, not all service to the Lord is pleasing to Him. Nor is everything that is called service really service to the Lord. There are a few things we need to understand in order to be successful in our service to the Lord.

First, we must belong to Him. That may seem obvious, but there will be many in the day of judgment who will think that they have been serving the Lord through their lives only to find out that He didn't recognize their work.

> *"Not everyone who says to Me, 'Lord, Lord,' shall enter the kingdom of heaven, but he who does the will of My Father in heaven. Many will say to Me in that day, 'Lord, Lord, have we not prophesied in Your name, cast out demons in Your name, and done many wonders in Your name?' And then I will declare to them, 'I never knew you; depart from Me, you who practice lawlessness!'"*
> *Matthew 7:21-23*

Wouldn't it be sad to serve the Lord and never really know Him? It might seem strange to us, but there are many people who serve the Lord that way. They have believed that service will gain salvation. They serve the Lord with strength and zeal because they think that the more they serve the better their chances for salvation. But it is very clear that salvation must come first. If you want your service to the Lord to be acceptable to Him, you must belong to Him.

The second thing we should know is that service to the Lord is only acceptable if we are clean. Someone once said that the Lord can use broken vessels, but He will not use unclean ones. Paul spoke to Timothy about people in the church who held on to pride and selfishness. He suggests that those who continue to serve the flesh or the world will be dishonored and therefore unfit for service. However, those who yield themselves to the Lord will be "vessels of honor."

> *Therefore if anyone cleanses himself from the latter, he will be a vessel for honor, sanctified and useful for the Master, prepared for every good work.*
> 2 Timothy 2:21

Does that mean that the Lord will only use us if our lives are perfect? Of course not. If that were the case, no service would ever be accomplished. No, it simply means that we are to be cleansed by His wonderful cleansing grace and sincere in our service to Him. If we hold on to sin, if we reject the Lord in our hearts, our service will not be acceptable. He wants clean vessels for His use.

Then, finally, we must be fully submitted to Him. We have talked before about the desire to serve the Lord in the flesh. We sit down with ourselves and decide just how we will serve the Lord. We will do our thing our way and then we will offer it to Him. The only problem with that is He may not have wanted us to do that in that way. It is poor service to serve without asking.

Think of it this way. Suppose we think of the Lord truly as our Lord and Master. Then we think of ourselves as His servants. Wouldn't it be foolish for a servant to bring the master some act of service that the master didn't want? There would be no blessing in an unwanted service. Suppose your paper boy decided to add to his service to you by ringing your doorbell when he delivers the paper. Would that be a blessing to you? Suppose your doctor decided to give you a shot you didn't expect for some disease you didn't even have. Would that be a blessing to you? Suppose the gas station sent a tow truck to get your car so they could fill it with gas as a service to you. Would that be a blessing to you?

You see, the true servant asks the master. He comes to the master in humility and asks how he can serve. This is the attitude we are to have. We ask Jesus what He would have us do and then do it in service to Him. Don't worry, if you ask in sincerity, you will find an answer at the right time. He may want you to wait for a while, or He may want you just to keep doing what you are doing, but He hears your prayer.

Like Paul, the true servant, operating under "serving grace," comes to the Master and seeks the Master's will. Then the servant trusts that the Master will call on him when the time is right and that the Master will provide everything that is needed to accomplish the act of service.

John Milton, after confronting his blindness, wrote words that capture the truth of serving grace: *"They also serve who only stand and wait."* Waiting on the Lord is also service to Him. We forget that we simply are to be available when He calls. We think that we must be always doing some great activity. Instead, the Master gives us time just for worship and praise. During those times of waiting, we can learn more about Him, and we can open our hearts more to Him.

The true servant is also willing to do something small, even something others might not notice. The nature of the task doesn't matter if it fulfills the command of the Master.

The well-known minister, Andrew Bonar, brought home a brick from his travels in the area of ancient Babylon. One Sunday he showed it to his congregation. He said that every brick in the temple from which it was taken bore the name of the king who was reigning at the time the structure was built. Making the application, Bonar said, "We must let everything we do bear the name of our King, the Lord Jesus Christ." Some time later, a woman came to the minister and exclaimed, "Those bricks. Oh, those bricks of Babylon!" Sensing the implication of her statement, he asked, "Did you find them while sweeping the floors?" "No," she said, "I found them while making the beds. You remember you said that everything we did should bear the name of our Savior. Well, shortly after that, I had to change the beds, a job I thoroughly dislike. So, I said, 'I will do this in the name of Jesus and for His glory!'"

This is one of the secrets Hudson Taylor discovered. He is credited with saying:

I used to ask God to help me. Then I asked if I might help him. I ended up asking him to do his work through me.

If some small task will fulfill the purpose of our Master, then it is just as important as any great task. As we yield ourselves to Him to serve Him His way, we find our service acceptable to Him. True joy of service comes when we realize that all our work, all our time and effort, is simply the use of our lives by His hand. C. S. Lewis reminded us that only God does the work of God:

> *When we talk of a man doing anything for God or giving anything to God, I will tell you what it is really like. It is like a small child going to its father and saying, "Daddy, give me sixpence to buy you a birthday present." Of course, the father does, and he is pleased with the child's present.*[4]

In other words, acceptable service to the Lord is the work of the Lord Himself as He uses us. We are the tools in His hands, ideally, with no wills of our own except to serve Him. This is true Christian service.

In order to serve Him the way we should, we need serving grace. This is what is spoken of in Hebrews:

> *Therefore, since we are receiving a kingdom which cannot be shaken, let us have grace, by which we may serve God acceptably with reverence and godly fear. Hebrews 12:28*

His grace will prepare us for service. His grace will lead us to the right service. His grace will enable us to do the work. His grace will do the work in and through us.

What is our part? "Reverence and godly fear." In other words, genuine submission to the King of kings and Lord of lords. To be available to Him. To be ready to be used by Him. To allow nothing to be in the way of our service to Him. This is serving grace... and even that is from Him.

****

[4] Lewis, Clive Staples. Mere Christianity. New York: HarperCollins. 2001. p. 143

PERSEVERING GRACE

There wasn't much money in 1932, so it was no time to buy a drugstore. Then grasshoppers ate all the crops in the region. This, in turn, was followed by a dust bowl, a long drought and temperatures for ten days straight of over 100 degrees. So, the drugstore seemed about to fold. Nevertheless, Ted and Dorothy Husted believed in God.

They asked themselves: "How can we get these people into the drugstore?" They said, "We'll put up some signs." So, they went 25 miles in each direction and put up signs that read, "Free Ice Water at the Wall Drugstore, Wall, S.D." They put up signs at 10 miles; and at 5 miles the sign read: "Hold on! It's Only 5 Miles to the Wall Drugstore and Free Ice Water." They got so enthusiastic that they even put up a sign at Albany, New York: "1725 Miles to the Wall Drugstore." Of course, druggists had been handing out free ice water for generations, but Ted & Dorothy were the first people who ever thought of advertising it. In 1981, they said they were giving away 20,000 cups of free water every day—that's in a town of 800 people. It remains one of the most spectacularly successful drugstores in the entire industry.

Why? Because they persevered. They kept going. They didn't give up. Their gimmick wasn't necessarily better than anyone else's. They just kept at it.

The people of the Lord are called to persevere. Of all the people of this world, we are the ones who know the end. Victory belongs to the Lord, and eternal victory is ours through Him.

Of course, in these days we have cause to wonder about that, don't we? Whether it is the shakiness of the economy or the dishonor of our leadership or the terrorist problem or whatever, we certainly see the world falling apart around us. We wonder what is going to happen, and we really don't have any answers. Many of God's people are troubled and don't know what to do.

The answer, of course, is to keep going. We must persevere. Perhaps the passage we remember best on this topic is what Paul wrote to the Galatians.

> *And let us not grow weary while doing good, for in due season we shall reap if we do not lose heart.*
> *Galatians 6:9*

Good is coming! Hang in there! But what happens when good is a long time coming? What happens when we begin to understand that the good won't come in our lifetime? What happens if we can't see the good coming at all?

Now, that isn't to suggest that I don't believe

the Scripture. I believe that "in due season" we will find that promised good. The problem is that many Christians don't feel the benefit of the promise. That doesn't make the promise less true. When we are working so hard to do right and we find difficulties at every turn, it just gets discouraging.

Certainly, Abraham could give testimony to the importance of persevering and trusting the Lord. Waiting for Isaac is an example of trusting in God's promise even though it takes a long time to come. He was a hundred years old before he saw the son of God's promise.

Yet, this makes me think of another man. He also had a word from the Lord, and for many years he watched for the word to be fulfilled. He watched, and he waited, but nothing ever happened. It was a true word from God, yet everything seemed to work against the promise. When would it come? How would it come? For so many years there was no answer.

But some of you might feel that kind of pressure today. You believe the word the Lord has given you. You believe the Scripture promises. The days just keep going, and nothing seems to change. You wait and wait, but nothing happens.

I want to offer some words of encouragement. I want to share with you the idea of *Persevering Grace*.

In those times of discouragement, when everything seems to be just one problem or barrier after another, when you seem to be working against the clock and losing time, you need persevering grace. When it seems like you might as well give up, that your hopes and dreams will never happen, you need persevering grace. When everyone around you is in a state of panic or confusion and the temptation to join them is strong, you need persevering grace.

Now, you will remember that we have said that grace is the wonderful, majestic, omnipotent Lord God reaching down to us in our hopeless state and fulfilling our needs. If we are called by Him to persevere, to keep doing His will no matter what, then we must call on Him for the ability to do that. There is nothing in us that wants to do His will in the first place and certainly nothing in us that will be able to keep going in the hard times. Any perseverance must come from Him.

Scripture offers an opposite to perseverance. It seems that there is a tendency, even among the people of God, to "faint in the midst of adversity." Since adversity increases as we become more separated from the world and its ways, the temptation to faint, to fall apart or fall down on the job, increases as well.

Faintheartedness is the opposite of perseverance. To faint means to fall down or fall back, to stop doing what you were doing. Those who belong to the Lord should not faint in serving Him or in doing right.

We are told that lack of perseverance, or fainting, is a sign of weak faith.

> *If you faint in the day of adversity, your strength is small.*

Proverbs 24:10

We are not to "faint in the day of adversity" because our faith should be strong enough to keep us going. In fact, faintheartedness is sometimes seen as a punishment from the Lord. There is a curse for those who fall away from serving the Lord.

> *'And as for those of you who are left, I will send faintness into their hearts in the lands of their enemies; the sound of a shaken leaf shall cause them to flee; they shall flee as though fleeing from a sword, and they shall fall when no one pursues.'*
> *Leviticus 26:36*

In other words, those who wander from the Lord will find in themselves not only a weakness of faith, but a general weakness that will cause them to faint in adversity. There will be no strength in them to stand against anything. They will find themselves afraid even if there is no truth to the rumors or the perception of danger.

Wars and rumors of wars. Troubles and rumors of troubles. We don't know what tomorrow will bring, do we? Will there be an economic collapse? Will there be wars? Will there be persecution for the people of God? Who knows?

What we do know is that faintheartedness is contagious. Panic spreads rapidly regardless of fact. Those who faint will likely take along others. I remember a story about a young people's choir where one of the young ladies, overcome by the stress and the heat, fell down in a faint. It wasn't long before another fell and then another. Soon the choir had to stop their performance because so many of their number had fainted.

When the people of Israel prepared to enter the Promised Land, the leaders knew that faintheartedness was contagious. That's why this command was given:

> *The officers shall speak further to the people, and say, 'What man is there who is fearful and faint-hearted? Let him go and return to his house, lest the heart of his brethren faint like his heart.'*
> *Deuteronomy 20:8*

In other words, you don't even want to be around those who are fainthearted because they may well drag you down, especially if you are not prepared.

But we are weak! We do fall back! Being strong is not easy for us. When we look at the enemies around us, when we think of all that appears to be expected of us, it seems almost normal to get a little faint.

The good news is that those who faint in the day of adversity can find the true source of power. Remember the story of Jonah? In the belly of the great fish, he cried out to the Lord. Later, when he wrote his account, he said:

> *"When my soul fainted within me, I remembered the LORD; and my prayer went up to You, into Your holy temple."*
> *Jonah 2:7*

When faintheartedness drives us to the end of ourselves, we may cry out to the Lord and find His strength. In fact, the only help we have in the day of adversity is from Him.

The remedy for faintheartedness, that which enables us to persevere, is *hope*. We keep going because of what we believe is promised, right? We trust that the Lord, who commanded our service, will bless our efforts in His time. That's hope. The Scriptures talk of two foundations for hope, the Word of God:

> *My soul faints for Your salvation, but I hope in*
> *Your word.*
> *Psalm 119:81*

And the Lord Himself, or perhaps we could say the character of God:

> *Happy is he who has the God of Jacob for his help,*
> *whose hope is in the LORD his God,*
> *Psalm 146:5*

Our hope is found in the faithfulness of our Lord. He is our Hope. He does not faint, Isaiah said. He is strong and wise and loving. He is wonderful and powerful and majestic beyond comparison. And, in His grace, He reaches down to us and fulfills our need.

Our relationship with the Lord is the key. This is what we have been seeing all along, isn't it? Those who wander from the Lord will find themselves becoming faint when trouble comes. Their relationship with Him is compromised, and they have no source of strength. So, they look to themselves and their own strength to save them. They have "fallen" from His grace.

> *You have become estranged from Christ, you who attempt to be justified by law; you have fallen from grace.*
> *Galatians 5:4*

They have fainted under the attack. They have fallen back, fallen down, and are unable to stand strong.

On the other hand, those who cultivate their relationship with the Lord have hope and will be able to stand in that difficult day. They keep their eyes on His faithfulness, and they know that they can keep going.

But how? That's always the question. How can we do this? There is a wonderful and simple answer.

We don't usually talk much about perseverance. Perhaps one reason we don't use the word much is because the Scripture doesn't use it much. Jesus told a parable about perseverance without using the word, but it also had this special application. There is a special call to perseverance in one specific area of our lives. That is prayer.

> *...praying always with all prayer and supplication in the Spirit, being watchful to this end with all perseverance and supplication for all the saints...*
> *Ephesians 6:18*

In other words, don't forsake prayer. Keep praying. Don't ever stop praying. That's the purpose of the parable Jesus told as well:

> *Then He spoke a parable to them, that men always ought to pray and not lose heart, saying: "There was in a certain city a judge who did not fear God nor regard man. Now there was a widow in that city; and she came to him, saying, 'Get justice for me from my adversary.' And he would not for a while; but afterward he said within himself, 'Though I do not fear God nor regard man, yet because this widow troubles me I will avenge her, lest by her continual coming she weary me.'"*
> *Then the Lord said, "Hear what the unjust judge said. And shall God not avenge His own elect who cry out day and night to Him, though He bears long with them? I tell you that He will avenge them speedily. Nevertheless, when the Son of Man comes, will He really find faith on the earth?"*
> *Luke 18:1-8*

When you and I stop praying, our relationship with the Lord seems to go on hold. The longer we fail to pray, the more distant we are from Him. We then find ourselves becoming afraid and anxious because we have no access to His wonderful strength and provision.

Pray for persevering grace. Pray for perseverance in prayer. Pray that the Lord would grant you opportunity and motivation to pray without ceasing. Persevering grace comes to those who pray.

Remember the man I mentioned earlier who had the word from the Lord? His name was Simeon. He waited many years faithfully without seeing any fulfillment. Year after year things only looked worse. No one seemed to care anymore. The Lord seemed to have forgotten His people.

Yet, it was the habit of this man to go to the Temple in Jerusalem to pray. He sought that wonderful grace-filled relationship with the Lord. One day, as he came to the Temple to pray, he met a man and a woman with a tiny baby, and Simeon knew that his prayers had been heard. He had persevered. The promise of God was true. He was to see the Messiah of God before his death and on this day a little baby named Jesus had been brought to the Temple for His circumcision.

> And behold, there was a man in Jerusalem whose name was Simeon, and this man was just and devout, waiting for the Consolation of Israel, and the Holy Spirit was upon him. And it had been revealed to him by the Holy Spirit that he would not see death before he had seen the Lord's Christ. So, he came by the Spirit into the temple. And when the parents brought in the Child Jesus, to do for Him according to the custom of the law, he took Him up in his arms and blessed God and said:
> "Lord, now You are letting Your servant depart in peace, according to Your word; For my eyes have seen Your salvation which You have prepared before the face of all peoples, a light to bring revelation to the Gentiles, and the glory of Your people Israel."
> Luke 2:25-32

Does perseverance pay off? Of course, it does. Our

Lord is faithful. His promises are sure. His love for us is amazing. His grace is sufficient.

DYING GRACE

A man had a checkup and then went in to see his doctor to get the results. The doctor said he had bad news and worse news for him, which did he want to hear first? The man was a bit disturbed and said he'd rather hear the bad news first. The doctor said, "The bad news is that you only have twenty-four hours to live."

At this the man jumped up distraught. He paced the doctor's office and complained, "Twenty-four hours to live? I can't possibly get my affairs in order that quickly. I can't believe this, it is incredible! What could be worse news than this?"

The doctor said, "Well, I was supposed to tell you this yesterday."

How many of us are prepared to die? If it were to come tomorrow, would you be ready? Those are sobering questions, aren't they? We don't like to think about death and dying. After all, we say, the message of the gospel is a message about life. When we think of the things of the faith, we should hear about good things not things like dying.

Yet, the process of dying, for a believer, can be a

time of great and effective testimony, if we are prepared. We will all die, unless the Lord returns first, but will we all be ready?

Even Christians don't like to think about death. There is something in us that wants to push death as far away as possible. No matter how often we are told that death is just a passage to the eternal and wonderful life God has in store for us, we still find it hard to think about.

Yet, what if we didn't die? What if we just kept going day after day, year after year, forever? Our bodies would continue to break down, perhaps, but we would not die. The struggles of this life would never end. We would never be free from sin and pain and fear. We would never experience life as it was meant to be for us.

Think about that. For thousands of years we would deal with corruption in leadership, with betrayed trust, with family struggles, with all the difficulties this world offers. The joys would become stale, and there would be less pleasure and more pain. Eternal life in this world would not be a blessing.

Our Lord understood that. When the first sin was committed, death was decreed for humankind. We usually think of it as a punishment, but I would suggest that it was not a punishment at all. Instead, it was the only way out of a broken world. The only way out is through, as they say, through death.

It seems that, as we get older, the holidays increasingly remind us of the reality of dying. Some of our friends or family are not with us this year because they have passed away. We remember grandparents or other family members who left a mark in our lives but are now gone. We celebrate traditions left to us by generations that have gone before us. We wonder who will be gone from us the next time we celebrate.

Death is real. None of us will avoid it, unless Jesus returns to take us away. Many generations have thought that they would be the ones who would be spared dying so they could rise with Him in the air, but none have been right so far. It is far more likely that we will die as all those before us have died. The only question is whether we will die well.

It has been my privilege to minister to many people before they died. I have been greatly touched by the confidence of those who have had a lifelong relationship with the Lord. Even as their memory fades, they often remember Him and His love.

I remember hearing about the last days of a young man who died of a brain tumor. They said that on his deathbed he recited Bible verses until he died. He didn't seem to know anyone or anything, but he knew the words of his Master.

How will we die? Will we die well? We should ask the Lord for *Dying Grace*. Of all the times in our life when we want Him to be in control, our final testimony seems most important. Our last words, our last actions, our last thoughts. What a blessing if they would all be His!

I have always liked the words of Moses as he addressed the people of Israel at the end of his life. He said,

"Behold, this day I am going the way of all the earth" Joshua 23:14

He understood that death was inevitable. He understood that all things must come to an end. David understood also and said much the same thing to his son Solomon as he gave his last instructions:

"I go the way of all the earth"

Fanny Crosby understood as she wrote her special song, *"Someday the silver cord will break, and I no more as now shall sing..."*

Those who trust in the Lord can look death in the face with confidence and even joy. They know that staying here isn't an option, nor would it be a blessing. To leave this world, no matter what kind of pleasures it represents, for the glories of Heaven is an easy thing for those who know their Master and trust Him.

You see, Heaven is real. There is eternal hope for those who belong to Jesus. There is eternal joy in the presence of the Lord. There is no more pain, no more tears, just as the Scripture says. Those who die in the Lord receive the blessing of Heaven.

As a young man, D.L. Moody was called upon to preach a funeral sermon. He hunted through the four Gospels trying to find one of Christ's funeral sermons without success. He found that Christ broke up every funeral he ever attended. Death could not exist where he was. When the dead heard his voice, they sprang to life. Jesus said, "I am the resurrection, and the life."

Life is the promise of our Lord, eternal life and eternal joy. This is His promise for those who will trust Him. We have nothing to fear.

Yet, many believers, men and women who say that they believe these things, are afraid to leave this world. They do everything they can to stay here, to avoid death. It is right, of course, for us to seek to serve the Lord as long as we can. We should not seek death, but we also should not be afraid of it. Many Christians are afraid of death.

That why we need *dying grace*. We have seen how He has called us, how He has saved us, how He has cleansed us, how He has done all these wonderful things in our lives. We have seen how He is ready to love others through us, to keep us faithful in our service, even to pray through us. All that we have in the Christian life is from Him. Now we see that even the end of our lives is His, and the ability to die well is a blessing of His grace.

There seems to be some risk in including a chapter about death in a book on grace. On the other hand, there are few things more universally important than understanding how to die.

You see, people who are prepared to die don't get that way just at the end. Moses walked with God and talked with Him. He spent a good portion of his life learning about the Lord and serving Him. David was the beloved of the Lord. His relationship with the Lord was the most important thing in his life. Fanny Crosby lived for the Lord long before she died. It wasn't something that happened at the end to make their passing easier. No, they were prepared. They had died already.

It may be fifty years before the Lord calls us home, or tomorrow. The timing doesn't matter. What matters is that we are prepared. And there is only one way to prepare for death.

The only way to prepare for death is to die. You see, the Bible speaks of two kinds of death, death to this life, which all human beings will share, and death at the cross, which only those who belong to Jesus will pass through.

The key to dying well is to surrender your life to Jesus Christ in advance. When we come to Jesus, we die. He takes us with Him, in Him, to die on the cross. Yes, this is a little hard to understand, but the Scripture is clear.

> *...knowing this, that our old man was crucified with Him, that the body of sin might be done away with, that we should no longer be slaves of sin.*
> *Romans 6:6*
>
> *I have been crucified with Christ; it is no longer I who live, but Christ lives in me; and the life which I now live in the flesh I live by faith in the Son of God, who loved me and gave Himself for me.*
> *Galatians 2:20*

If you have given your life to Jesus, you can be assured that He took you with Him to the cross. You died. The only thing left is for you to live as though you have died.

Yes, I know, that's a little strange, but we are dead,

dead to sin, dead to this world, dead to the flesh. Again, this is the firm and clear teaching of the Scriptures.

> *Likewise you also, reckon yourselves to be dead indeed to sin, but alive to God in Christ Jesus our Lord. Romans 6:11*
>
> *And those who are Christ's have crucified the flesh with its passions and desires.*
> *Galatians 5:24*
>
> *For you died, and your life is hidden with Christ in God.*
> *Colossians 3:3*

You and I are dead to sin and dead to the flesh. Neither of them will ever have power over us again. The Scriptures also say that we are no longer citizens of this world; this world's ways no longer are our ways. As far as the realm of the evil one is concerned, we are dead.

What does it mean that we are already dead? It means that the things of this life and this world no longer hold us with their attractions. It means that we can deny the passions of the flesh because dead people have no passions of the flesh. It means that we have already left the things of this life behind. It means that we can leave this world with peace and joy in our hearts.

Why are we afraid to die? Because we aren't quite sure that what is offered to us by the Lord is as certain or as wonderful as what we have here. We are still trying to hold on to the things of this life. We are still identifying with the realm of sin and the flesh. We are afraid to die, because we find it hard to die to what we know.

But those who belong to Jesus Christ are called to live as those who are dead and to die as those who will live forever. Think about that. If we have already left behind the things of this world, there is nothing we need to release when this life ends. We can rejoice in anticipation of the wonderful fulfillment of the glorious life eternal, as we look toward the end of this life.

You see, those who have already died will never die again. Christians only die once. When we surrender our lives to Jesus Christ, we will never die again.

> *Now if we died with Christ, we believe that we shall also live with Him, knowing that Christ, having been raised from the dead, dies no more. Death no longer has dominion over Him. For the death that He died, He died to sin once for all; but the life that He lives, He lives to God. Likewise you also, reckon yourselves to be dead indeed to sin, but alive to God in Christ Jesus our Lord.*
> *Romans 6:8 -11*

When you and I came to Jesus Christ, we died in the same way as He died. Just as He can never die again, the promise is that we will never die again. When we came to Him, we died, and there is no more need for death.

So, understand this: Dying grace isn't just that which we need in order to die. Dying grace is what we need to live. Pray that you would be filled with dying grace. Pray that you would be able to leave this world behind even during the days you remain here. The more you and I can release the things of this life now, the easier it will be when the time comes for us to leave. In the same way, the more we learn to cling to Jesus Christ and enjoy our relationship with Him now, the more joyful it will be in that day when we will be in His presence forever.

Perhaps the one person who understood this idea of grace the best was Paul. He certainly shows his great wisdom in the book of Galatians. As he faced the end of his life, he knew that he had released all the things of this world. All he had in his possession was Jesus, and all he ever wanted was more of Jesus. That's why he could say with joy and confidence:

> *For to me, to live is Christ, and to die is gain. Philippians 1:21*

Those are the words of a Christian. If I stay, I will enjoy Jesus, and He will be all I need. If I die, I will have more of Jesus. Either way is acceptable to me. That's the joy of dying grace.

MYSTERIOUS
GRACE

"A watched pot never boils."
*"If a tree falls in the forest when no one is
there to hear, does it make a sound?"*

Well, we know the watched pot will eventually
boil, although probably just when you decide to look
away. The tree falling is a harder problem, isn't it?
We say, of course it makes a sound. If you sneak to a
nearby spot, you could hear it, but that changes the
equation. So would a recorder of some kind because
it would be a listening device. With no way for you
to hear, there would be no way to prove the sound except that every other falling tree makes a sound.

We often tend to answer mysteries by inserting
what we know. Years ago, a philosopher asked if we
could prove that the sun would rise in the morning.
The only real answer is that we must assume it will
because it has done so consistently for a very long
time. Proving something for the future is difficult.

A man named Schrodinger discussed with Einstein the problems presented in quantum physics. I don't have the time or the knowledge to really explain his conundrum, except to say that he brought up a question about a cat in a box. If the cat is in a sealed box with a source of poison that might or might not kill the cat, and you have no way of observing the cat, then the cat could be either dead or alive. The poison might have killed the cat, or it might not have. Without observing, you will never know. But once you observe, the question goes away. If you don't observe, the cat could be, in a sense, both dead and alive.

That discussion and further actual experiments revealed something physicists call the "observer effect." They have found certain phenomena that seem to change based only on whether someone is watching. Like the child in the kitchen near the cookie jar, it matters whether mom is watching. Otherwise, what happens might remain a mystery.

We have a love/hate relationship with mysteries. God has given us permission to search out truth. We study science and medicine and even history because we want to know what's right. Why do certain things happen? How do they happen? Can we make them happen? We tend to dissect almost everything in creation because we want to understand. It is the "glory of kings," says Proverbs 25:2, "to search out a matter." When we don't have to worry about our next meal, we may have time to study a mystery.

At the same time, we don't really like not knowing the answers, especially when those answers affect us. The remote for the television seems to be loaded with mysteries. Maybe it is fun for some people to play with the things and understand their features, but most of us just want to be able to turn the television on, change the channels, and adjust the volume. We don't really want the mystery.

As we walk through our lives, we would like to know what's happening and why, wouldn't we? But we don't. We don't know when we are going to die, for example. We don't know what next year will bring. We don't know what Heaven will be like. We don't know a lot of things. And we might like to know these things.

But we are left with mysteries. For several years I studied the Bible to understand the end-times prophecies. I didn't get into it like some did, but I thought I understood the general flow of things. But the 80's came and went, with all their turmoil and evil. Then the 90's, and soon we were well into the 2000's. And, even though evil grew and nations fought and the church compromised, the Lord still didn't come. Despite all the charts and systems and books and videos, we still don't know the time of His coming. It will happen, somehow and someday, but we are stuck with a mystery.

It does the church no honor and the world no good for us to fight about mysteries. There are many mysteries in theology. Which church has it right? Probably none of them. We think our system makes more sense than theirs, but how can we be sure? The Scriptures guide all of us, but we don't get enough information to settle the mysteries. As we commonly say, there will be many questions answered at the end.

Or not. Maybe some things will always be mysteries. Maybe God will not choose to tell us everything we want to know, or maybe we will cease to puzzle about such things in the light of all the wonders of glory. We'll see.

Grace is mysterious. The cause-and-effect formulas of those who still live under the law will never solve the questions. The charts, the books, the systems will all fail. There may be things we will never understand.

And, even though the Lord has allowed us to search out mysteries and has made us with inquisitive minds, it is arrogant for us to think that we can understand everything. God is great and His creation is great. There isn't time in our short lives to understand all the wonders of nature, but we think we should be able to understand that part of life that affects us. Maybe not. Maybe the wonders of our own lives, our own days, are too much for us as well.

> Come now, you who say, "Today or tomorrow we will go to such and such a city, spend a year there, buy and sell, and make a profit"; whereas you do not know what will happen tomorrow. For what is your life? It is even a vapor that appears for a little time and then vanishes away. Instead you ought to say, "If the Lord wills, we shall live and do this or that." But now you boast in your arrogance. All such boasting is evil.
> James 4:13-16

You see, when you and I came to Jesus, we entered a relationship with a real Person. He is a Person every bit as much as we are. The Scriptures reveal God to us in stories so we will understand He is not just an idea or a force. He is a Person. He relates to us as a person.

People are confusingly complex. The more you know someone, the more you realize that you will never fully think like that person. Couples who have been together for decades still surprise each other with ideas, values, and responses. Just about the time you think you have someone figured out, you will be shocked to find that you have more to learn.

We learn about people by observing and connecting. We discover that people are very much alike, at least in some ways. So, we are able to categorize and have a basic sense of understanding. That allows us to function in a crowded society. The culture today speaks strongly against stereotyping, but stereotyping is an unfortunate extension of this categorizing we do to understand others. The problems come when we assume that individuals are bound by those categorizations. Groups may or may not live in predictable ways, but individuals—persons—are not so limited. When we look at a person and judge or anticipate their actions based on our stereotypes, we do that person a disservice. We disrespect the personhood of that individual. He or she is far more complex than our stereotype could ever be.

Nor can we extrapolate from an individual to a group. Creating a stereotype, or any categorization, based on our interaction with or observation of an individual or a small group usually leads us to wrong, even hurtful, conclusions.

A person is a wonder, a unique creation of the Lord. Everything from backgrounds, nationalities, memories, life experiences, to chemical interactions within the body combines to make one person different from every other person. We don't know what another person is thinking, no matter how confidently we might predict his or her next move. We guess based on our observations and categorizations, but we dare not depend on our accuracy. People will surprise us.

It would be an insult to try to reduce a spouse or child to a chart of cause-and-effect processes. I might expect that my wife will respond a certain way to a suggestion, but to create a system where I can plug in variables and predict her response would deny the marvel of her individuality, her personhood. And, of course, no matter how detailed my system, it would still fail. Not all the time, but enough to remind me that she is different from me.

Yet, we treat the Lord as though He could be influenced, or His actions could be predicted according to theological systems. Praying certain prayers are said to guarantee certain results. Certain actions, good or bad, bring predictable responses. Some teachers specialize in creating these structures within which God must operate. Proof texts from Scripture and logical formulas chart God's decisions. And they fail over and over.

I'll never forget hearing Chuck Smith of Calvary Chapel on the radio one day as he said, "Every time I have given God a deadline, He has missed it." Chuck learned that God is a Person. Contrast that with another well-known preacher I saw on the television. He was on his knees, pounding on the floor, and demanding that God fulfill a promise this man claimed. In his mind, God was bound by a certain verse or word and could not operate in an alternate way.

You and I might be able to force the people in our lives to do certain things, but we cannot force God to behave according to our will. We draw closer to our Lord when we see Him like us, but we too easily forget that He is not like us. Jesus lived in our world and suffered in ways we suffer, but He is a Person in many ways so different from us that we will never fully comprehend His glory. In other words, if you and I can't even understand the ways and the thinking of the people in our lives, how can we expect to understand the mysteries in the mind of God?

And He reminds us of that truth.

> *"For My thoughts are not your thoughts, nor are your ways My ways," says the LORD. "For as the heavens are higher than the earth, so are My ways higher than your ways, and My thoughts than your thoughts.*
> *Isaiah 55:8-9*

I have heard scholars teach that these verses don't mean quite what they say. Yet, even if we didn't have these words, we would have the stories of Scripture and the experience of our own lives to know that God is beyond our predictions and control. C. S. Lewis said that the great Lion was not tame. Even if we limit our desire for understanding to the things of our own lives, we find that the complexities are too much. Only the mind of God knows us. Perhaps God does not reveal the answers to us because they are too much for us to get our small minds around.

God is a Person. He has ideas and purposes and desires. He has knowledge and power we do not have. He has no sin. He is more than us, but we are enough like Him to know that we are connected by His love for us.

Jesus, who is God, is a Person. Complex and wonderful, He has His own thoughts and values and goals. We blaspheme if we consider Him anything less than a Person. That means we allow Him to be Him.

So, if we follow Jesus, if that is what the Christian life is all about, then we might not always know where we are going. Someone has said, "I don't know where I am going, but I know who I am following." As we read the gospels, we see that Jesus and the disciples walked from place to place. The disciples were following Jesus. They visited among themselves and wondered about what He said before. We get the picture of Jesus out in front. They didn't know what was coming next. They might have had a general idea of the purpose of their journey, getting to Jerusalem for the feast perhaps, but they didn't know when He might stop. And, if He stopped, He might do something they were not prepared for. He might ask them a question or heal someone or ask the disciples to do something for Him. Their day would have been unpredictable.

"Unpredictable" may be a good word for the authentic Christian life. You and I write down our plans for tomorrow, perhaps even for the year. Then we watch to see what really happens. Our days are filled with mystery—because we follow a Person.

Paul suggests that we will know more in Heaven than we do now. Today our vision is clouded by the imperfect light in which we walk. We are creatures of the light walking in the land of darkness. We see, but we don't see everything.

> *For now we see in a mirror, dimly, but then face to face. Now I know in part, but then I shall know just as I also am known.*
> *1 Corinthians 13:12*

Those who came before us, under the Old Covenant, saw even less. They looked for a Messiah who didn't come, generation after generation. They lived through evil leadership, cruel conquerors, and empty days. But they had a promise given by a Person. There was much they did not understand, a great many mysteries, but they looked to the Person of their faith.

> *These all died in faith, not having received the promises, but having seen them afar off were assured of them, embraced them and confessed that they were strangers and pilgrims on the earth.*
> *Hebrews 11:13*

And those who "died in faith" without receiving

the promises in their earthly lifetimes saw the fulfillment of their hopes in the Person of Jesus Christ. It
happened just as the Lord had promised—in His way
and His time.

So how do we follow when we don't know where
we are going? We keep our eyes on the One we are
following—and we trust Him. That's what faith is.
Knowledge is not faith. Predictability does not lead
to faith. Faith is not knowing, not controlling, and
still walking.

> *Now faith is the substance of things hoped for, the*
> *evidence of things not seen.*
> *Hebrews 11:1*

Jesus is God's grace for your heart. The love of God
came to us in the Person of Jesus Christ. Everything in
our relationship with the Father resists the formula,
the mathematical equation. It is not a blueprint, but
a relationship. And a relationship is filled with mystery. Faith is how we live in that relationship of mystery.

There is a part of me, as a pastor, that would like
to give assurance in times of trouble, to say that I
could guarantee a certain outcome. Even if it meant
a certain formula of behavior or prayer. Struggling
people want to know what to do and when the struggle will end. But that would be so much less than
what they could have. My job has never been to have
the answers but to connect hurting people with the
One who does have those answers. He alone has the
love and the power and the wisdom to walk with

them through their days. I am not the person they need, nor is my wisdom sufficient for their hearts.

But I find myself longing for the same kind of answers. There is hope, but that hope is sometimes hard to see. The evil of our day increases, pain and disappointment so often accompany age, and we face a future we cannot control. Where is our hope? Paul understood this:

> *For we were saved in this hope, but hope that is seen is not hope; for why does one still hope for what he sees? But if we hope for what we do not see, we eagerly wait for it with perseverance. Likewise the Spirit also helps in our weaknesses. For we do not know what we should pray for as we ought, but the Spirit Himself makes intercession for us with groanings which cannot be uttered.*
> *Romans 8:24-26*

If we try to place our hope in a certain outcome or even a certain path, we will have no assurance. The only hope that is certain is that found in the Person of Jesus. If we look to Him in faith, we can allow the mystery.

Jesus understands our hearts. "The Spirit," Paul says, "helps in our weaknesses." He prays with us and for us, even when our hearts groan. When the frustration grows and the answers do not come, we have a Person who walks alongside us. If our picture of Jesus is in front leading, then our picture of the Spirit must be of One who walks beside us. He lifts us up, speaks words of encouragement, and keeps us connected to the One who leads. The imagery of the Scripture is so beautiful if we remember that it teaches us about relationship, rather than formula. The Father has a wonderful plan of love for us, the Son leads us on the paths of righteousness so that plan is fulfilled, and the Spirit walks alongside as our comfort and encouragement.

> *Now He who searches the hearts knows what the mind of the Spirit is, because He makes intercession for the saints according to the will of God.*
> *Romans 8:27*

Paul completes his thoughts on this with one of the most encouraging portions of Scripture.

> *And we know that all things work together for good to those who love God, to those who are the called according to His purpose. For whom He foreknew, He also predestined to be conformed to the image of His Son, that He might be the firstborn among many brethren. Moreover whom He predestined, these He also called; whom He called, these He also justified; and whom He justified, these He also glorified. What then shall we say to these things? If God is for us, who can be against us? He who did not spare His own Son, but delivered Him up for us all, how shall He not with Him also freely give us all things? Who shall bring a charge against God's elect? It is God who justifies. Who is he who condemns? It is Christ who died, and furthermore is also risen, who is even at the right hand of God, who also makes intercession for us. Who shall separate us from the love of Christ? Shall tribulation,*

*or distress, or persecution, or famine, or naked-
ness, or peril, or sword? As it is written: "For Your
sake we are killed all day long; We are accounted
as sheep for the slaughter." Yet in all these things
we are more than conquerors through Him who
loved us. For I am persuaded that neither death nor
life, nor angels nor principalities nor powers, nor
things present nor things to come, nor height nor
depth, nor any other created thing, shall be able to
separate us from the love of God which is in Christ
Jesus our Lord.*
Romans 8:28-39

If you are going through a time that seems con-
fusing, keep your eyes on Jesus. Nothing will separate
you from His love for you. No struggle, no enemy, no
personal weakness, no sin can pull you out of His presence. You long for answers that don't seem to come,
but trust in the One who knows and who loves you.
Your path may not be like that of others. Your answers may not come from a book or a teacher. But He
is with you. Trust Him.

There is mystery in the Christian life, but it is the
mystery of grace. Surrounded by the love of God, we
walk through unpredictable and uncontrollable days,
trusting that He leads us in ways that are good and
right. *Mysterious Grace* means individual purpose and
love.

Mysterious grace means you are in relationship
with a real Person.

PURE GRACE

Have you seen movies where people had to walk across long old rope bridges with rotting boards under their feet? Every step is dangerous; every board is treacherous. The natives still use the bridge, but the newcomers don't know which boards are strong and which are ready to break. At any moment they could be thrown onto the rocks below. There is usually some enemy in close pursuit, and the hero must get across the bridge as quickly as possible. He or she steps uncertainly, testing each board, then suddenly one breaks, and the hero is almost killed. Fortunately, the ropes are strong enough, and the hero can make it across.

When Paul wrote to the Galatians, he was both sad and angry. He had presented a strong message of grace, but the people doubted that message. From the beginning of the letter, Paul accuses the people of embracing "another gospel," even though he says there is only one. So concerned was he about the changes in what they taught that he suggested they were leaving the faith altogether. In his mind, there was one message, one gospel, one truth about the work of Jesus on our behalf.

So, what were the Galatians doing? Well, first, they still considered themselves believers and followers of Jesus. The only problem was that they were taking to themselves the laws of the Jews. Paul reminds them that he was a leader among the faithful Jews, that he knew the Law, and that the gospel he taught did not require keeping the Law. Jesus had fulfilled the law for us. But the Galatians listened to those who told them they had to keep the law in order to be right with God.

One of the reasons God chose Paul must have been that Paul could explain what it meant to come out from under the law because we are under grace. The disciples had trouble understanding this. They were Jews who had been taught that certain rituals and behaviors defined them. Paul had also been taught this but saw so clearly the distinction between law and grace. He knew the law had served to reveal their bondage to sin, while grace revealed the freedom Jesus had purchased for them.

Paul considered this return to the law a bewitchment, a lie from the evil one to entrap the hearts of the people. They would find only the old comparisons and discouragement. The Jews who returned to the law would find bondage again. The Gentiles who adopted the law would find a new bondage. Paul said that the law was a curse from which Christ set the people free.

The parts of the law the Galatians were adopting are not laid out in a list for us. We assume that things like dietary restrictions, circumcision, and Sabbath rules were being taught and accepted. One of the purposes the Jews saw in the law was separation from other people. It doesn't seem inconsistent with the letter to suggest that these believers were observing rituals and behaviors for that purpose. Jewish believers and false teachers brought their traditions and expectations into the church.

But the law does not mix with grace, according to Paul. The law is a trap, a weak link that leads to failure. The law could only provide the cracked boards on that long bridge across the chasm. And stepping on those boards, assuming they would be safe, would be a false and dangerous hope. Trusting in rituals or rules would certainly be trusting in those unsafe boards.

I am reminded of the old story of the man who went into battle wearing a cross, a crucifix, a star of David, a star and crescent, and a rabbit's foot. He just wanted to be sure he was covered.

Believing in everything is the same as believing in nothing. Mixing the message of grace with the message of law nullifies the earthly benefits of grace. When Paul says that the Galatians have "fallen from grace," he does not mean they have lost their salvation. Our salvation is by grace whether we acknowledge it or not. If we trust in Jesus, we experience our salvation. But adding requirements, rules and rituals, will weaken our faith, not strengthen it. We will begin again to try to trust in ourselves and our efforts. The old anxieties, insecurities, and doubts will come rushing in.

Paul said it would be like the old entanglement.

> *Stand fast therefore in the liberty by which Christ has made us free, and do not be entangled again with a yoke of bondage. Indeed I, Paul, say to you that if you become circumcised, Christ will profit you nothing. And I testify again to every man who becomes circumcised that he is a debtor to keep the whole law. You have become estranged from Christ, you who attempt to be justified by law; you have fallen from grace. For we through the Spirit eagerly wait for the hope of righteousness by faith. For in Christ Jesus neither circumcision nor uncircumcision avails anything, but faith working through love.*
> *Galatians 5:1-6*

To "fall from grace" is to embrace the old bondage, to push the benefits of grace aside and take back the burden of the law. The assurance you enjoy as you trust that all the requirements for your salvation have been fulfilled in the person and work of Jesus Christ goes away if you begin to trust in other things. If, suddenly, you decide to go back under the law, trusting in your ability to keep the rules and rituals, that assurance can only be as strong as your obedience. The forgiveness you felt when you realized that Jesus took all your sins—past, present, and future—to the cross to be washed away by His blood once and for all will no longer feel as certain. As you focus on your obedience, seeking to supplement His work, you will never again be sure that you have done enough. The joy of your freedom in Christ, following Him alone as your Friend, vanishes as the new anxieties become your bondage.

The peace of grace comes as we focus on Jesus. The grace of God is not just an idea, nor a stage of Christian growth, but a Person. That Person loves us and has sacrificed to reconcile us to God. He understands our weaknesses and is our strength. He knows our sin and is our cleansing. Jesus is God's grace for our hearts.

Paul's message to the Galatians is clear: grace is all you have, and grace is found only in Jesus. The law has nothing more to offer those who belong to Jesus. He has completed all the requirements for our salvation, and our eternal life is assured. Trying to add to what Jesus has done is a trap.

Jesus warned his disciples against the "leaven of the Pharisees." As far back as human history goes, the people used yeast to bake bread. Someone has suggested that the yeast culture was discovered accidentally, since it is a natural organism. Leaven, the yeast-cultured dough, can be carried for many years from one batch of bread to the next. In a positive sense, the yeast bacterium is a fermentation agent for food and drink. In a negative sense, you could say that the yeast is an infection. Once in a welcoming medium, the yeast multiplies and produces the gases that make bread rise and ale ferment. Once in the dough, the yeast cannot be removed easily.

Yeast was such a normal part of baking that unleavened bread was unusual. To have unleavened bread, a baker had to protect the dough from contamination. Any small amount of dough left from previous baking might infect the new dough. Sometimes yeast bacteria came from exposure to the air. So, the dough had to be isolated if it was to be kept unleavened.

In the same way, the message of grace must be protected from the infection of legalistic ideas and expectations. The leaven of the law is insidious.

> *Now when His disciples had come to the other side, they had forgotten to take bread. Then Jesus said to them, "Take heed and beware of the leaven of the Pharisees and the Sadducees." And they reasoned among themselves, saying, "It is because we have taken no bread." But Jesus, being aware of it, said to them, "O you of little faith, why do you reason among yourselves because you have brought no bread? Do you not yet understand, or remember the five loaves of the five thousand and how many baskets you took up? Nor the seven loaves of the four thousand and how many large baskets you took up? How is it you do not understand that I did not speak to you concerning bread?—but to beware of the leaven of the Pharisees and Sadducees." Then they understood that He did not tell them to beware of the leaven of bread, but of the doctrine of the Pharisees and Sadducees.*
> *Matthew 16:5-12*

Jesus used a common and easily remembered illustration to teach the disciples about the dangers of contamination. They were to listen closely to what He taught and not bring into the gospel the infection of the Pharisee's message. The Pharisees taught how to be acceptable to God by our actions. They not only taught the law but added to it a variety of extensions designed to make people even more spiritual. Everything the Pharisees taught focused on the law and human performance. When Jesus came to tell the people of the Father's love, the Pharisees were not ready to receive the real message of God's heart.

But the message of Jesus was that the Father would provide all that was needed to restore our relationship with Him. He sent Jesus to be the one sufficient sacrifice for our sins and the only way to eternal life. Jesus revealed the Father's power and provision when He fed the five thousand at one point and the four thousand at another. The disciples were not to worry about bread, they were to look to Jesus and trust in Him.

The leaven of the law was the old way of thinking. Bringing it into the new was not only dangerous but would result in a product that was not desirable. When the requirement for unleavened bread was given for Passover and for the grain offering, it would illustrate the need to protect the truth. Yes, the message of the unleavened bread was the haste in which the Hebrews left Egypt, but the illustration was ready to be used by both Jesus and Paul much later. It would have been easily understood by all the people. Mixing leaven with the dough will not result in the unleavened bread desired.

So, Paul tells the Galatians:

> *A little leaven leavens the whole lump.*
> *Galatians 5:9*

The whole message of grace can be compromised by a little law. In fact, if we are to carry the illustration further, a little law will grow to become a lot of law, and the strength of a pure message of grace will be lost.

Now, let's see what this looks like. Suppose you attend a church that proclaims the freedom and peace that comes from an understanding of grace. The leadership tells people they don't have to worry about their sins separating them from the love of God in Jesus. They don't have to be afraid of losing their salvation or feel continued shame for past sins. But then the pastor or the church leaders say that a person must tithe in order to be blessed by God. That same church may tell you that your anger separates you from Jesus and you must forgive in order to be forgiven. If you dig under the surface, you will probably find more "little" things. The message of grace is prominent, but the message of performance and law is there as well.

What will people focus on in this church? Most people will enjoy the message of grace and feel good about it, but they will want to know more about the rules. How much anger is too much? Is frustration the same as anger? What if you have a good reason to be angry? How much is a tithe? Do I tithe before or after taxes? If I give more than a tithe, will God give me even more? If I forgive my abuser, but still remember and cry, have I forgiven enough? What if he/she isn't sorry? If I struggle with forgiving him/her does God struggle with forgiving me? On and on and on.

The "little law" naturally turns us toward our performance of the rules and rituals. Judgment on performance makes sense to our flesh, to the way we learned life apart from Jesus. So, the flesh, which is still a serious influence on the way we think, will look for ways to perform better and will seek assurance based on that performance. As long as our relationship with God depends on doing certain things, no matter what Jesus has already done for us, we will turn our focus to those things.

In many ways, the mixed message of grace and law is the most dangerous for the believer. To use the language of grace, with the assurances of grace, while adding simple "common-sense" requirements to the message, is to bait a trap from which many will never escape. The church that proclaims Jesus plus rules or rituals—in order to be acceptable to God—will bring those who have tasted freedom back into bondage.

Two things must be said here. First, those who return to the law do not lose their salvation. The mixed message results in the loss of assurance and peace, rather than eternal life. As noted earlier, "falling from grace" means losing the benefits of knowing the truth of grace in this life. The danger and effect are not insubstantial. Those who add to grace the rituals or rules of law sacrifice both freedom and peace. They return to the fear and anxiety they had before they learned the sufficiency of Christ. But they do not lose their salvation. Salvation comes through grace, no matter how much people try to add to it.

Second, there is still a place for a church to proclaim the dangers of sin. Sin may no longer be able to separate us from Christ and all He has done for us, but it will still hurt us and others. There are many reasons for a church or a teacher to warn people about sin that have nothing to do with salvation or negating the work of Christ. Just because you hear a message against sin does not mean you are hearing a mixed message.

Paul spent a good amount of his letter space warning believers about sin. He cared about their peace, but also about the peace of the churches. He knew the dangers of comparisons and compromises. He spoke to those who added law to grace in the same way he spoke to those who ignore the dangers of sin because they are under grace. Being under grace does not make sin less evil or dangerous.

Paul addressed this concern with words that remind us of the idea of "falling from grace."

> *Therefore strengthen the hands which hang down, and the feeble knees, and make straight paths for your feet, so that what is lame may not be dislocated, but rather be healed. Pursue peace with all people, and holiness, without which no one will see the Lord: looking carefully lest anyone fall short of the grace of God; lest any root of bitterness springing up cause trouble, and by this many become defiled; lest there be any fornicator or profane person like Esau, who for one morsel of food sold his birthright. For you know that afterward, when he wanted to inherit the blessing, he was rejected, for he found no place for repentance, though he sought*

it diligently with tears.
Hebrews 12:12-17

To "fall short of the grace of God" is different from falling from grace, but only in timing, as Paul used the concept. As we said before, to fall from grace was to return to the law and lose the assurance and joy of salvation. To fall short of grace is to be less than we could be under grace. It is possible for sin to entangle believers in ways that seem to rob us of our identity and unity.

Two kinds of people: like Esau, those who were never saved; and the recipients of the letter, those who are saved but are in danger of losing unity with other believers and looking like they are not saved.

Reality Check!

Where will you hear or read a message of pure grace? The uncompromised, unencumbered, message of God's grace can only be found in His message to us. Our salvation is an experience of pure grace, whether we understand it that way or not. The Bible's message is one of pure grace, if we could separate the traditions or burdens the church has placed on it. The truth is that the message of grace filtered through the flesh of any teacher or any earthy tradition will be mixed with performance.

Even though the dangers of the mixed message are great, able to snatch away the peace and assurance of the believer, that mixture will be the only thing heard from the pulpit, read in the books, or even interpreted from our own reading of the Bible. I would never claim to teach pure grace, nor would I believe anyone who claimed to teach pure grace. The flesh is too pervasive, too familiar. The flesh will take the message of grace and twist it so subtly that it affirms and welcomes even as it mixes in expectations and performance.

I believe in pure grace, inasmuch as I understand it. I don't live it, nor do I see it around me. I don't expect to hear it in any church over time. Yes, a single message can tell the truth of what Jesus did and how it does not depend on our work, but other teachings of the church, other messages, may compromise that message with expectations and suggestions that obedience is what purchases God's favor.

Believers should look only to Jesus for pure grace, just as we look to Him alone for perfect love. Those who come to Jesus will find grace and love as gifts.

There are churches that use the words of grace: freedom, victory, new covenant, and more, without actually teaching grace. I have heard teachers say that they were 90% grace and 10% law, as though that was somehow a valid message of grace. Others have said that grace is the key and we earn grace by obeying. Still others express gratitude for God's grace and encourage their followers to go out to deserve that grace. In most of these mixed messages, the law is still central and still binding. Grace words are popular in today's culture, but mixed with law, they are weakened.

There are others that try very hard to promote a pure message of grace. Yet, they seem to forget that message when they speak on giving or service or even hope for the future. The teachers might not even consider the connection between the message of grace and the practical things of the church or daily life. Subjects like tithing or obedience so benignly connect to the law that many who believe in grace still preach a message that binds people to performance.

The believer must seek the direct leading of the Lord. Jesus will lead through the Spirit as we seek Him. He will lead us away from sin. He will lead us into good works. These are dynamic aspects of living under grace. Yet, they are not law-based expectations. Our salvation is neither gained nor lost by our performance. Nor is the love God has for each of us.

Some through history and in a few groups today have suggested that pure grace means salvation separate from human interaction. It is true that God offers His gifts apart from human contribution. In other words, there is nothing we can do to earn or deserve the gift He gives. It is not the result of our good living or even our good believing. It is God's action out of God's motivation and initiative. He offers it to us freely, even as we are His enemies in our hearts.

At the same time, it is a gift, not an encumbrance. He gives it freely but does not force it on anyone. Some teach that the grace of God for salvation has been applied to all who have ever lived, regardless of their faith or response to God's love. All are saved, they say, because of what Jesus did on the cross. Some even say that all are saved simply because God the Son became human. There are fine points of theology and anthropology in this discussion, but the mystery of God's grace includes our free response.

The grace of God comes to us through faith, our personal response to what God offers. There may be many ways to respond, but God does not force anyone. The response of one may not look like the response of another, but the free acceptance of God's love in Jesus opens the door to saving grace in our hearts. "Grace through faith," Paul said.

Yes, there are aspects of grace available to all people. The gift is freely offered to all. The cross is sufficient to wash away all sins of all people. The call goes out across time and place to any who will hear. And those who seek peace with God will find Him. But no one is forced into Heaven, and no one who does not want what is offered will be made to take it.

Pure grace, as taught by the Scriptures, works through faith. God may deal with people who have little or no access to Christian teaching in ways of His choosing, but He will not force anyone. He will offer, in whatever way He wants, and they will be expected to respond. Always the desire is for them to be saved. Always the offer is free. Always the offer is pure grace. Always the offer is Jesus.

It is not necessary to deny the teachings of the Scripture that personal response by faith is part of our salvation. Universalism, by whatever name or description, is not the logical extension of pure grace.

Grace is a gift, one that can be rejected.

CONCLUSION

By faith, we step out of the old life of performance and duty and into the new life of grace. We bow before our Savior carrying only our need. He looks on us with love and reveals Himself in our lives with power. When we come with nothing but our need—no bargaining, no offering, no merit—we are in the right position to receive.

Our need is great. Sin, and the flesh's attempts to survive in a broken world, have damaged every part of us. We need a Savior who is active in every area of our lives, because we need grace in every area of our lives. Any idea of grace that doesn't touch the most practical parts of our day is too weak for our need.

The list of practical "graces" could be very long. Parenting grace, marriage grace, preaching grace, friendship grace, daily work grace, and more. Some have assumed that we are on our own to struggle through these daily challenges. Some have been taught not to "bother" the Lord with these things. Yet, these are the very things that drag our hearts to despair and fill our minds with anxiety.

Life is daily, someone has said. Few people have

the luxury to study the details of doctrine and theology. If grace remains in the "ivory towers," the people of God shuffle from one crisis to the next with little connection to the power and love of their Lord. Money, relationships, health, jobs, kids: these things occupy our minds and hearts, threatening our energy and enthusiasm even for the things of the faith. Unless the things of the faith are intimately connected to the things of our daily lives.

The old song asks, "Does Jesus Care?" Does He care when my heart is breaking? Does He care when I am afraid? Does He care when people hurt me? But, even more, can He do anything for me? Does the fact that He cares make a practical difference in my life?

Yes, Jesus cares. And, yes, He cares enough to act in your life. Paul said that the Lord told him His grace would be sufficient in times of struggle. The strength of the Lord would be Paul's strength.

Among grace teachers there is a strong aversion to anything that looks or smells like a formula. We have good reason for that. There is no magical incantation, no reciprocal deal, and no corporate privilege that brings either salvation or the activity of God's grace. There is a Person.

But how we come to that Person is important. Sometimes we come as the leper, with our ugliness and weakness exposed for all to see. Sometimes we come like Peter, reaching up to Jesus as we sink into the abyss. Sometimes we come as the father of the tormented boy, weak in faith and hope. We come to bow down before Him in our need. He is our Hope. He alone has our answers and deliverance.

Jesus is God's grace for your heart. He stands ready to give you whatever He asks of you. When He calls you to be faithful, expect Him to give you faith. When He calls you to love, expect Him to love through you. When He calls you to change, expect Him to be your strength.

Ask Him.

CPSIA information can be obtained
at www.ICGtesting.com
Printed in the USA
LVHW041411111119
636960LV00003B/921/P

9 781702 545518